8th Workshop on Challenges in the Management of Large Corpora (CMLC-8)

Marseille, France
11 – 16 May 2020

Editors:

Piotr Banski
Adrien Barbaresi
Simon Clematide
Marc Kupietz
Harald Lungen
Ines Pisetta

ISBN: 978-1-7138-1257-9

Printed from e-media with permission by:

Curran Associates, Inc.
57 Morehouse Lane
Red Hook, NY 12571

Some format issues inherent in the e-media version may also appear in this print version.

Association for Computational Linguistics
209 N. Eighth Street
Stroudsburg, Pennsylvania 18360

Phone: 1-570-476-8006
Fax: 1-570-476-0860

acl@aclweb.org

Additional copies of this publication are available from:

Curran Associates, Inc.
57 Morehouse Lane
Red Hook, NY 12571 USA
Phone: 845-758-0400
Fax: 845-758-2633
Email: curran@proceedings.com
Web: www.proceedings.com

LREC 2020 Workshop
Language Resources and Evaluation Conference
11–16 May 2020

8th Workshop on Challenges in the Management of Large Corpora (CMLC-8)

PROCEEDINGS

Editors: Piotr Bański, Adrien Barbaresi, Simon Clematide, Marc Kupietz, Harald Lüngen, Ines Pisetta

Proceedings of the LREC 2020
8th Workshop on Challenges in the Management of Large Corpora
(CMLC-8)

Edited by: Piotr Bański, Adrien Barbaresi, Simon Clematide,Marc Kupietz, Harald Lüngen, and Ines Pisetta

For more information:
European Language Resources Association (ELRA)
9 rue des Cordelières
75013, Paris
France
http://www.elra.info
Email: lrec@elda.org

Introduction

In order to satisfy the information needs of a wide range of researchers across a number of disciplines, large textual datasets require careful design, collection, cleaning, encoding, annotation, storage, retrieval, and curation. This daunting set of tasks has coalesced into a number of key themes and questions that are of interest to the contributing research communities: (a) what sampling techniques can we apply? (b) what quality issues should we be aware of? (c) what infrastructures and frameworks are being developed for the efficient storage, annotation, analysis and retrieval of large datasets? (d) what affordances do visualisation techniques offer for the exploratory analysis approaches of corpora? (e) what legal paths can be followed in dealing with IPR and data protection issues governing both the data sources and the query results? (f) how to guarantee that corpus data remain available and usable in a sustainable way?

Over the past years, the CMLC workshop series has gathered researchers interested in these long-standing topics while also willing to address newly developing trends in the field. At each meeting, we also made sure to reserve space for national corpus project reports. In the year 2020, we expected our meeting to be co-located with the LREC conference, which had unfailingly hosted the previous CMLC events, from Istanbul through Reykjavík, Portorož and Miyazaki. Unfortunately, due to the spreading COVID-19 pandemic, the May date had to be cancelled. Nevertheless, we are hereby offering the present volume of proceedings, with thanks to the contributing Authors and heartfelt gratitude to the Reviewers. Whether we will be able to suggest an alternative date or mode for the meeting, time will tell. The relevant information will be placed on the CMLC-8 homepage at http://corpora.ids-mannheim.de/cmlc-2020.html .

P. Bański, A. Barbaresi, S. Clematide, M. Kupietz, H. Lüngen — May 2020

Organizers:

Piotr Bański, IDS Mannheim
Adrien Barbaresi, Berlin-Brandenburg Academy of Sciences
Simon Clematide, Institute of Computational Linguistics, UZH
Marc Kupietz, IDS Mannheim
Harald Lüngen, IDS Mannheim

Program Committee:

Laurence Anthony, Waseda University, Japan
Vladimír Benko, Slovak Academy of Sciences
Felix Bildhauer, IDS Mannheim
Sonja Bosch, University of South Africa
Dan Cristea, "Alexandru Ioan Cuza" University of Iasi
Damir Ćavar, Indiana University, Bloomington
Tomaž Erjavec, Jožef Stefan Institute
Stefan Evert, Friedrich-Alexander-Universität Nürnberg/Erlangen
Johannes Graën, University of Gothenburg, Pompeu Fabra University
Andrew Hardie, Lancaster University
Serge Heiden, ENS de Lyon
Miloš Jakubíček, Lexical Computing Ltd.
Dawn Knight, Cardiff University, UK
Natalia Kotsyba, Samsung Poland
Michal Křen, Charles University, Prague
Sandra Kübler, Indiana University, Bloomington
Gaël Lejeune, Sorbonne Université
Paul Rayson, Lancaster University
Martin Reynaert, Tilburg University
Laurent Romary, INRIA
Kevin Scannell, Saint-Louis University
Roland Schäfer, FU Berlin
Serge Sharoff, University of Leeds
Irena Spasic, Cardiff University
Marko Tadić, University of Zagreb, Faculty of Humanities and Social Sciences
Ludovic Tanguy, University of Toulouse
Dan Tufiş, Romanian Academy, Bucharest
Tamás Váradi, Research Institute for Linguistics, Hungarian Academy of Sciences

Table of Contents

Conference Program

Addressing Cha(lle)nges in Long-Term Archiving of Large Corpora
Denis Arnold, Bernhard Fisseni, Pawel Kamocki, Oliver Schonefeld, Marc Kupietz and Thomas Schmidt

Evaluating a Dependency Parser on DeReKo
Peter Fankhauser, Bich-Ngoc Do and Marc Kupietz

French Contextualized Word-Embeddings with a sip of CaBeRnet: a New French Balanced Reference Corpus
Murielle Popa-Fabre, Pedro Javier Ortiz Suárez, Benoît Sagot and Éric de la Clergerie

Geoparsing the historical Gazetteers of Scotland: accurately computing location in mass digitised texts
Rosa Filgueira, Claire Grover, Melissa Terras and Beatrice Alex

The Corpus Query Middleware of Tomorrow – A Proposal for a Hybrid Corpus Query Architecture
Markus Gärtner

Using full text indices for querying spoken language data
Elena Frick and Thomas Schmidt

Challenges for Making Use of a Large Text Corpus such as the 'AAC – Austrian Academy Corpus' for Digital Literary Studies
Hanno Biber

Czech National Corpus in 2020: Recent Developments and Future Outlook
Michal Kren

Adding a Syntactic Annotation Level to the Corpus of Contemporary Romanian Language
Andrei Scutelnicu, Catalina Maranduc and Dan Cristea

Proceedings of he 8th Workshop on Challenges in the Management of Large Corpora, pages 1–9
Language Resources and Evaluation Conference (LREC 2020), Marseille, 11–16 May 2020

Addressing Cha(lle)nges in Long-Term Archiving of Large Corpora

Denis Arnold, Bernhard Fisseni, Paweł Kamocki, Oliver Schonefeld, Marc Kupietz, Thomas Schmidt
Leibniz-Institut für Deutsche Sprache
R5 6–13, 68161 Mannheim, Germany
{arnold | fisseni | kamocki | schonefeld | kupietz | thomas.schmidt} @ ids-mannheim.de

Abstract

This paper addresses long-term archival for large corpora. Three aspects specific to language resources are focused, namely (1) the removal of resources for legal reasons, (2) versioning of (unchanged) objects in constantly growing resources, especially where objects can be part of multiple releases but also part of different collections, and (3) the conversion of data to new formats for digital preservation. It is motivated why language resources may have to be changed, and why formats may need to be converted. As a solution, the use of an intermediate proxy object called a *signpost* is suggested. The approach will be exemplified with respect to the corpora of the Leibniz Institute for the German Language in Mannheim, namely the German Reference Corpus (DeReKo) and the Archive for Spoken German (AGD).

Keywords: long-term archival, legal issues, metadata, format migration

1. Introduction: Three Challenges

The current paper investigates long-term archival (LTA) for large corpora, specifically corpora that are constantly extended and contain material where the conglomerate of commercial interests, intellectual property rights and privacy rights constitutes a non-trivial problem; we call them **growing corpora**. We focus on three aspects of archiving growing corpora which are related to changing resources, and in our opinion, can be approached by using tombstones or, preferably, signposts.

While we restrict our attention to growing corpora, all aspects apply to other kinds of corpora as well, but generally to a different degree. In the interest of space, we leave it to the attentive reader to judge the applicability.

Caron et al. (2017) discuss their solution in the context of the Open Archival Information System model (generally abbreviated: OAIS, see CCSDS, 2012; for an overview, see also the 4th chapter by Oßwald in Neuroth et al., 2009), and specifically the aspect of dealing with the ingest of a submission information package into the archive. In the OAIS, an *edition* is characterized by change in the content (e.g., Oßwald only speaks of additions), while a *version* is the result of a migration (cf. CCSDS, 2012, p. 1-9; § 5.1, esp. §5.1.3.4 Transformation). In this sense, while initially motivated by transparently dealing with editions, the current approach tries to integrate versions and editions into a common model.

Reproducibility in science in general and reuse of data in particular have been recognised as important goals over the last years, also connected to the adoption of the term and concept of *open science* (cf. for an overview Fecher and Friesike, 2014) and the publication and wide-spread adoption of the FAIR principles (Wilkinson et al., 2016). To maintain reproducibility of a documented scientific procedure, it also is necessary to maintain the access to some form of the data. This is in immediate conflict with the removal of data. Surprisingly, while the change of data regarding formats is generally considered in the context of preservation (cf. an example for research data Conway et al., 2011), we have found no example that considers the change of data sets due to legal issues.

One aspect that distinguishes growing corpora from others is that for legal reasons, it may be necessary to remove or modify part of the data. In long-term archival (see, e.g., Digital Preservation Coalition, 2015; Neuroth et al., 2009), this case is generally neglected, as it is normally assumed that data will stay unchanged. To remain as close to the spirit of LTA as possible, one will still want to deliver some useful information when someone tries to retrieve the removed objects. This is especially important since it is reasonable to assume that a researcher will not expect that data referenced with some form of persistent identifier has been altered. To our knowledge, only Caron et al. (2017) have considered the deletion of objects in LTA. They describe a 'tombstone' which steps in for objects that needed to be deleted for legal reasons. Systems like Fedora Commons or DSpace allow for removal of resources and provide tombstone objects.[1] We will discuss the differences between these and our approaches below.

Another aspect is parsimonious representation of data in corpora with many releases: Objects may be referenced in different releases and resources. Corpora that are curated in projects where the corpora are constantly extended and published in frequent releases will have many (unchanged) objects in common across different releases. Furthermore, an object may belong to different collections. Generally, a digital long-term archive will avoid storing the same digital objects multiple times. Keeping only one copy per object ensures that there is no confusion about the state of an object and storage space is not wasted, especially when objects are considerably large.

The third and last aspect is specific to long-time preservation: It is unforeseeable if and when a given file format may become deprecated. But once this is the case, the archive will have to migrate the respective files to the new format and make them accessible along with the original files. This can be seen as a departure from the original model, which states "[...] that the new archival implementation of the information is a replacement for the old" (CCSDS, 2012, p. 1-11).

To explain the proposal, we distinguish the notions of *conceptual object* (CO) and *logical object* (LO) (see chapter 9 by

[1] https://wiki.lyrasis.org/display/FEDORA4x/RESTful+HTTP+API; https://wiki.lyrasis.org/display/DSDOC6x/Functional+Overview

Stefan Funk in Neuroth et al., 2009).[2] A CO can be realized in different LOs, for instance an audio recording (CO) can be realized in files of different audio formats (LO).

The first two cases, i.e. removal and and versioning primarily concern changes of conceptual objects – although the changes will be mirrored in LOs –, while the case of format conversion only concerns logical objects. This observation will form the basis of our technical proposal.

1.1. Background

The Leibniz Institute for the German Language (IDS) is building up a long-term archiving repository for linguistic data. Current work is focusing on the development of appropriate ways of ingesting the IDS's own corpora of written and spoken language. Both can be viewed as exemplars of large and growing corpora: The German Reference Corpus DeReKo (Kupietz et al., 2010, 2018) has been built at IDS since its foundation in the mid-60s (Teubert and Belica, 2014). It currently contains 46.9 billion tokens (Leibniz-Institut für Deutsche Sprache, 2020) corresponding to 56 GB disk space (without automatic annotations) and is used by more than 40 000 German linguists world-wide, primarily via specialized analysis platforms, such as COSMAS II (Bodmer, 2005) and KorAP (Bański et al., 2013). The Archive for Spoken German (AGD; Schmidt, 2017) hosts around 80 corpora of spoken language. The digital available corpora are published via the *Datenbank für Gesprochenes Deutsch* (Schmidt and Gasch, 2019). While much smaller than their written counterparts in terms of number of documents or tokens of (transcribed) text, they can also be viewed as large corpora because they comprise large digital audio or video files. For example, the 1 113 recordings of the BOLSA study (Lehr and Thomae, 1987) make up for altogether 2 833 hours of audio. Stored as mono WAV files with a sampling rate of 48 kHz, they occupy around 1 TB of disk space. For the latest version of the FOLK corpus (Schmidt, 2016), the textual data amounts to around 2.5 million transcribed tokens (less than 0.5 GB), whereas the archived media data (stereo WAV, 48 kHz for audio, MPEG-4 in a resolution of 1 980 × 1 080 for video) is also around 1 TB.

1.2. Legal Aspects

There are several possible scenarios where parts of large corpora intended for long-term archiving have to be deleted for legal reasons. Three legal frameworks seem to be of particular relevance here: intellectual property (IP), data protection and criminal law.

Intellectual Property

Firstly, concerning IP, it is important to note that language data are, for the most part, protected by copyright. As such, their use (i.e. reproduction and communication to the public) is lawful only in one of two cases: (1) a permission (license) has been obtained from the right holder or (2) the use is covered by a statutory exception or limitation (e.g. for teaching and research). In both cases, long-term archiving may be impacted.

A license can be granted for limited duration only, and once it comes to its term, the work can no longer be lawfully used. Technically speaking, it does not have to be deleted, but any further copying (even in a computer's memory) would amount to copyright infringement. Although from the user's point of view it is advantageous to use licenses that are not limited in time (or, rather, are granted for the whole duration of copyright), such as Creative Commons licenses, right holders cannot be forced to grant them. In practice, it is usually the case that the longer the licence period, the less likely it is that the licence will be granted, or higher fees may be charged, or both (see Kupietz et al., 2014, for a more detailed discussion of the trade-offs). In the case of DeReKo, the typical duration of commercial licenses is one year, while donated licenses are almost always unlimited in time.

A license can also be revoked by the licensor – usually because the right of revocation is specifically provided for in the license itself, in which case, of course, the stipulated modalities (e.g. prior notice) would have to be respected. Creative Commons licenses, for example, terminate automatically upon any breach of the license's terms. It is also possible, albeit in very limited cases, that the statute grants the right holder the right of revocation (i.e. the license can be revoked even if it does not stipulate so). Under German law, for example, an exclusive license can be revoked if the work is not used by the licensee (§41 UrhG[3]). More interestingly, still under German law, the author has the right to revoke a license 'for changed conviction' (§42 UrhG), i.e. when he decides that the work no longer reflects his conviction. In this case, the author has to adequately compensate the licensee for the revocation, and if in the future he decides to use the work again, he shall grant a new license to the licensee 'on reasonable conditions'. Exceptionally, the right of revocation for changed conviction can also be exercised by the author's heirs; then, however, it would require a proof that the author would have exercised exercised the right prior to his death. Upon revocation, whether on contractual or statutory grounds, the licensed data can no longer be lawfully used.

In the case of DeReKo, many licenses are explicitly revocable at any time with a period of a few weeks. Since the 2000s at the latest, a corresponding addition to the license conditions has often proved necessary in order to be able to conclude license agreements at all and in a reasonable time. So far, however, no licensor has made use of his right of revocation.

Statutory exceptions may seem to provide for a more stable ground for long-term archiving, but it is not always the case. It should be kept in mind that the exception may simply not allow for long-term archiving (such as the current data mining exception in German law – §60d UrhG), and even if it does, it may simply cease to apply at some point, or be replaced by a different, stricter norm (even though in the past decade or two the trend seems to be towards broadening the scope of statutory exceptions). Moreover, albeit very rarely, an exception may come with an 'expiry date' – this is the case of exceptions introduced in German law by the UrhWissG[4] (covering such uses as teaching, research, data mining and uses made by libraries), which will cease to apply at the end of February 2023 (although they are expected to be either maintained by the legislator, or replaced by other similar exceptions. Therefore, when long-term

[2] Funk (chapter 9 in Neuroth et al., 2009) also distinguish level of *physical object* which, however, is not immediately relevant for our current discussion.

[3] Act on Copyright and Related Rights (Gesetz über Urheberrecht und verwandte Schutzrechte (Urheberrechtsgesetz, UrhG)

[4] Gesetz zur Angleichung des Urheberrechts an die aktuellen Erfordernisse der Wissensgesellschaft

archiving is based on statutory exceptions, it is of the essence to stay informed about the developments in the legal framework, and adjust the archiving policy accordingly.

Data Protection

Another legal framework that crucially impacts long-term archiving is data protection; the most important source of data protection law is the famous General Data Protection Regulation (GDPR) which entered into application in the European Union on 25 May 2018.

First of all, it should be mentioned that when the corpus contains personal data (which is not unlikely to happen, taking into account the large scope of the notion), archiving for an undefined (and potentially unlimited) duration may simply not be an option. Storage limitation (the principle according to which personal data can be kept for longer than necessary to achieve the purposes of the processing – Article 5(1)(e) of the GDPR) is one of the fundamental principles governing the processing of personal data under the GDPR. However, the GDPR allows for derogations from this principle when the processing is carried out solely 'for archiving purposes in the public interest', or for research or statistical purposes (Article 89 of the GDPR). To be able to qualify for the derogation, however, the processing has to be subject to 'appropriate safeguards' such as e.g. pseudonymization. The rules regarding these purposes of processing remain largely country-specific – in Germany, at the federal level, processing for research purposes is governed by §27 of the BDSG[5], archiving in the public interest by §28, and 'appropriate safeguards' are listed in §22 of the same Act.

Even if the storage limitation principle with its derogations is observed, some data may still have to be deleted on the grounds of data protection. When the processing is based on consent of the data subject (which, alongside 'legitimate interest' is probably the most common ground for the processing of personal data in language corpora), the consent can be withdrawn at any time (Article 7(3) of the GDPR). The withdrawal has no retroactive effect (i.e. the processing based on consent prior to its withdrawal does not 'become unlawful'), but any further processing should stop (although it is possible to resume processing on a different ground, e.g. based on legitimate interest).

However, if the data is processed on the ground of legitimate interest, the data subject may still exercise the right to object (Article 21 of the GDPR), in which case the processing should stop, unless the controller (the person or entity who defines the means and purposes of the processing) demonstrates 'compelling legitimate grounds' for the processing which override the interests, rights and freedoms of the data subject. The right to object does not apply to processing for research purposes, or for the purpose of 'archiving in the public interest' (Article 89 of the GDPR, §§ 27–28 of the BDSG).

Finally, the data subject may also exercise his right of erasure (Article 17 of the GDPR), commonly referred to as 'the right to be forgotten'. This right is not limited even when the processing is carried out for research or archiving purposes (unless it 'seriously impairs' these purposes); however, perhaps contrary to the common belief, the conditions for exercising this right are in fact very strict, and in practice seem to require some sort of prior violation of the GDPR on behalf of the controller.

[5] German Federal Data Protection Act (Bundesdatenschutzgesetz vom 30. Juni 2017 (BGBl. I S. 2097))

Perhaps most importantly, the data subject may request erasure if the data minimisation principle has been violated, i.e. the data are no longer necessary to achieve the purpose of the processing. This ground can be successfully used while requesting erasure e.g. from search engines, and possibly also from large, publicly accessible corpora. It is worth noting that if the request for erasure is well-founded, the controller shall also make reasonable steps (including technical measures) to inform other controllers who process the same information, so that they can also proceed with the erasure.

Criminal Law

Last but not least, criminal law, and more specifically the rules regarding defamation and defamation-related offences (slander, libel, insult...), may also require deletion of some parts of large corpora. This is especially relevant for newspapers or other press materials.

Since national rules may vary significantly (there is no harmonised law of defamation at the EU level), we will use § 186 of the German Criminal Code for illustration purposes. The text provides that whoever disseminates a fact related to another person which may defame him or negatively affect public opinion about him, is punished with a fine or imprisonment for up to one year (when the offence is committed by dissemination of written materials, the penalty increases to two years). Apart from that, the claimant may also obtain an injunction (i.e. a court order for the defendant to stop disseminating the material), even preliminary (i.e. applicable even before the final decision on the merits of the case is made by the court). Needless to say, a defamation claim, even ill-founded may lead to (at least temporary) deletion of parts of long-term archived corpora.

In the case of DeReKo, injunctions are by far the most common reason for the removal of individual texts, with about two incidents per week. The obligation to remove the texts is also stipulated in the license agreements with the right holders. There is a consensus within the German linguistic community that the removal of individual texts is unavoidable and typically irrelevant with respect to linguistic findings and should not pose an insoluble problem in terms of reproducibility of research results, which is reflected in the guidelines on legal aspects of handling corpora of the German Research Foundation DFG (Deutsche Forschungsgemeinschaft, 2015, p. 19), quoted here from its English translation:

> Regarding the still existing problem of persistence of research data, there is a certain pragmatic consensus within the scientific community: text deletions because of personality rights should be considered acceptable also epistemologically, since the replicability of important and methodically valid research results does not depend on individual texts. What is probably more important is de facto the organizational effort that can be caused by individual deletions. It is recommended to factor this into project costs in advance, if possible. (Wildgans et al., 2017, p. 20)

The three frameworks presented above may to a limited extent be derogated from by laws on public archives, such as the Bundesarchivgesetz or Landesarchivgesetze in Germany (so-called *Löschungssurrogat*), or Code du patrimoine in France.

However, apart from them being heavily country-specific, their application is usually limited to 'official' registries or other documents of key importance for public administration, or to archiving by specifically designated institutions. Therefore, it is our opinion that the relevance of such laws on public archives for long-term archiving of language corpora is very limited and so they fall outside of the scope of this paper.

1.3. Versioning of COs

There are two cases in which COs change, only one of which constitutes a veritable challenge. The other one can be seen as unproblematic.
The unproblematic case arises when a resource is published in a new version, e.g. containing more annotations, but also correcting mistakes that will stay accessible in the previous version. The long-term archive will in this case simply issue a new version of the CO and the old version stays intact and accessible. There is a certain conflict of interests here: On the one hand, it may be interesting to users to see that there is a new version of an CO; on the other hand, integrating this information into the archive would most evidently be possible changing the metadata, a measure which evidently goes against the general guarantees of long-term archival. We suggest that in this case the latter point far outweighs the former: It is not necessary to point to the new version in the long-term archive and make changes to metadata. However, it is by perfectly admissible from an LTA perspective to point to old versions from the new ones – as long as the latter are archived after the former have been, as is normally the case. To improve usability, the presentation layer of the archive can invert these links without integrating them into the metadata proper.
The interesting case is when parts of a corpus must be altered; this generally occurs due to legal reasons: An alternative version of the respective CO and its LOs must be created, or the CO must even be deleted completely. In any case, the old version will no longer be accessible.
Caron et al.'s focus are single packages of digitised documents (images, text files) rather than growing, hierarchical corpora and partial modifications. Based on the OAIS terminology explained in our first section, they determine whether there is a new version or a new edition as follows (see their figure 3): Disregarding ingest failures, a modification or deletion of data (in their case, e.g., improved imaging) leads to a new version, while additional content or modification of metadata leads to a new edition.

1.4. Pointing to the Converted

Finally, it may happen that a certain file format falls out of use. For instance, in the area of video formats, Apple has retired its QuickTime format in macOS 10.15 (Catalina). In the area of text annotation, SGML (ISO8879:1986, 1986) has given way to XML (Bray et al., 1997). To anecdotically trace one of our migration paths: DeReKo used SGML/CES between 1999 and 2005, and was consequently converted to an XML-based format (for the history and the decisions involved, see Lüngen and Sperberg-McQueen, 2012), first based on the TEI's P3 recommendations (Sperberg-McQueen and Burnard, 1999), later converted to TEI P5 (Burnard and Bauman, 2020), the customization of the annotation is called I5. Similarly, in the area of spoken language annotation, the IDS is in the process of switching to the new ISO standard ISO-24624:2016 (ISO, 2016) for new annotations, s, and has also converted old annotations from a variety of formats including SGML, HTML and plain text. Also, the tools developed at the IDS, especially the EXMARaLDA family (Schmidt and Wörner, 2014)) are being adapted to work with this format.
One can argue that the older SGML and XML formats are still usable, but the modern formats provide much better interoperability at the current time. So while formats used in long-term archival are generally selected to minimize the chance of complete obsolescence or loss of readability, it may still be preferable to provide additional formats that are more readily supported by contemporary software. In this case, the original LO is not completely replaced, but it may be preferable to deliver an object in another format if one queries for the CO. Again it is inconvenient and misleading to modify the metadata of parent resources, as conceptually, not the CO but only the files realizing it have changed.
An important question is reversibility of transformations. For formats like video, where we store lossily compressed data, a transformation would probably not be reversible (CCSDS, 2012, p. 5-6f), as transcoding would introduce new compression COs. In case of the conversion of DeReKo from SGML to XML (cf. Lüngen and Sperberg-McQueen, 2012), however, the migration was reversible in the sense that all old data could be losslessly translated back. I5 has evolved further (as of this writing, the latest version is from 2020-03-05)[6] and accommodates features for new kinds of text (such as computer-mediated communication), new data may not be retranslatable to the old format. This effect of the migration path illustrates a further complication regarding growing corpora.
With respect to the OAIS model, we can model this as three cases: (1) First, the conversion is merely a change of the Dissemination Information Package (DIP), or (2) alternatively, it may constitute a migration, namely a a transformation (CCSDS, 2012, §5.1.3.4). By keeping the original data, we partly transcend the OAIS model.

2. Signposts: Dealing with Modified or Deleted Data in a Transparent Way

2.1. Example: Removing / Modifying Data

In DeReKo, the structure of the corpus has three levels: *corpus* (i.e., subcorpus), *document* and ultimately *text*. What the corpus and document levels correspond to, depends on the text type. For newspapers, for example, a year volume corresponds to a 'corpus' and a month to a 'document'. It is in newspaper and magazine documents that a removal may occur due to injunctions for privacy reasons. We have not yet had a case where a whole volume had to be removed.
For reasons of work effort, we have to retract the whole corpus release archive in case an injunction occurs. The next release archive of DeReKo, however, will contain a modified version of the document: We generally remove the body of a *text*, marking it as a gap in the XML annotation. (For technical reasons, it is necessary to have a `<div>` element after the `<gap>`.) Often, it is possible to keep the title of an article if it does not give away personal information.

[6]Information on the current state of the format can be found at https://www.ids-mannheim.de/kl/projekte/korpora/textmodell.html

```
<text>
    <body>
        <gap reason="injunction"/>
        <div type=""/>
    </body>
</text>
```

Figure 1 – An XML tombstone in IDS's I5 format, which is a selection of the TEI P5 recommendations. An injunction leads to a <gap> in the document.

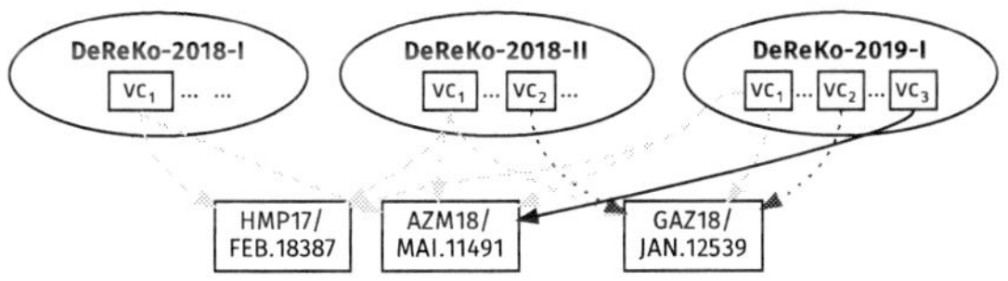

Figure 2 – Visualisation of the relationship between DeReKo releases, virtual sub-corpora and texts. DeReKo contains texts that are not only part of one corpus, but many (virtual) corpora. Considering the versioning, we find that text can be part of many different versions of many corpora.

2.2. Example: Versioning

Figure 2 shows the relationships between the DeReKo corpus releases DeReKo-2018-I – DeReKo-2019-I, three persistent virtual corpora $vc_{1,...,3}$, respectively initially defined on one of the releases, and three texts.[7] Based on DeReKo-2018-I, vc_1 was intensionally defined, already containing the texts HMP17/FEB.18387 and AZM18/MAI.11491. With DeReKo-2018-II, GAZ18/JAN.12539 was added to vc_1 because the text matches the intensional definition of vc_1. In addition, based on DeReKo-2018-II, vc_2 was defined, containing the text GAZ18/JAN.12539. Based on DeReKo-2019-I, then vc_3 was added, containing AZM18/MAI.1149. You can see here that texts in DeReKo can belong to many different corpora so that the removal of texts can have complex consequences.

2.3. General Discussion

Growing corpora are generally structured hierarchically, consisting of several subcorpora. The general approach is to model this as a containment relation, where the record of a parent resource refers directly to its constituent objects and also indicates specific information on the data, such as the file type. As Broeder et al. (2012) point out, the metadata should specify the MIME type, file size and potentially checksums, etc. In case of data removal, it is then possible to either modify the parent resource or to replace the object with a 'tombstone' which indicates removal of the original data (see fig. 3). This is what is suggested by Caron et al. (2017), but also implemented in systems like DSpace and Fedora with their tombstone features.[8]

[7]Note that virtual corpora are a key concept of DeReKo's *primordial sample* design (Kupietz et al., 2010). They can be defined extensionally by a list of corpus, document or text IDs or intensionally, for example as *All available texts originating from "Der Spiegel" since the year 2000.*

[8]https://wiki.lyrasis.org/display/FEDORA4x/RESTful+HTTP+API; https://wiki.lyrasis.org/display/DSDOC6x/Functional+Overview

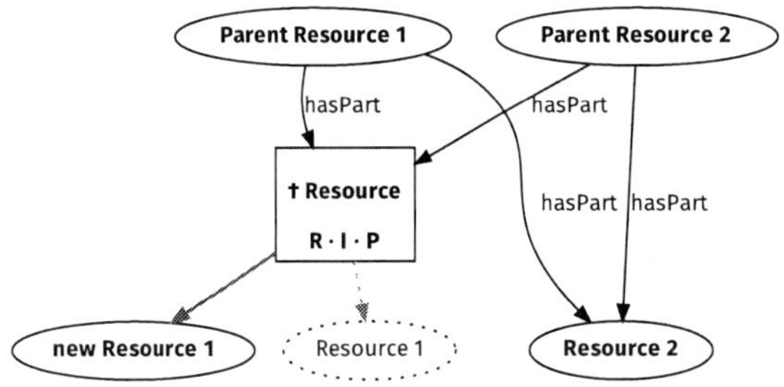

Figure 3 – A tombstone replaces a resource that has departed.

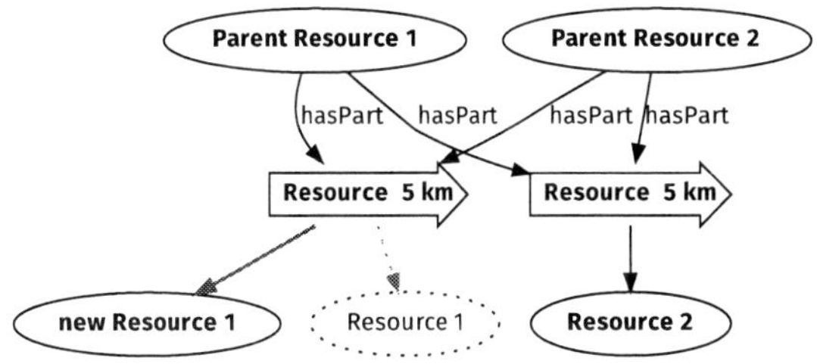

Figure 4 – A signpost just points to any resource – dead or alive!

However, this approach has several drawbacks: If it was possible before to address the removed object, e.g. by using a persistent identifier (PID), then only modifying the parent resource is insufficient, as it leaves the respective PID dangling. Therefore we now consider how to successfully implement the latter approach, namely the tombstones: We take it for granted that a tombstone object should be machine-readable and discernible as a tombstone rather than mere different data. In the general case, a replaced object may have represented an arbitrary kind of data, such as audio or audiovisual recordings or textual data. It is then evident that the tombstone object will not be of the same type as the replaced object. Hence, removal of objects has the effect that all metadata referring to the objects have to be modified as well by updating all information relating to the LO. Especially in the domain of growing corpora, this often constitutes a non-trivial change, and it again violates the precept of long-term archival that data will not be modified.

We suggest here that by introducing one layer of indirection, we can minimize modifications by introducing an intermediate object. It is customary to take the LOs which realize an CO to be the constituents of collections, and also to be referenced in metadata. We suggest that instead of the digital object, the CO be considered the referent of persistent identifiers, and its representation functions as a proxy or signpost. We use *CO* as an ontological category, and speak of *signpost* when we refer to a digital representation in a repository system. The general idea (see fig. 4) is to defer the specification of information on LOs representing a constituent CO to the signpost of the CO rather than to the record of the parent resource. The parent resource only contains general information on the CO and refers to the signpost. While the signpost can turn into a dead-end – analogously to a tombstone –, all data referring to it remain unchanged, which is advantageous in all cases mentioned above.

3. Signposts: Outsourcing the Object Metadata into a Separate Entity

If all metadata of parent resources only refers to the signpost, the metadata need not be modified if a resource becomes unavailable, or new formats are added.

As indicated above, there are consequences for metadata for parent resources, however, compared to the traditional approach: These metadata may only contain very general information on an CO then, e.g. whether it contains audio, audiovisual or textual data, but not whether it is a WAV file, an MPEG4 file with H.265 with AAC audio etc. If the metadata were this specific, a modification of the signpost would not be possible, and it would ultimately not offer added value.

The following features should be encoded in a signpost; we will make this more concrete in section 3.2.

the overall state: whether or not the CO is available.

the files: the files realizing the same CO; the description should include a MIME type, check sums and all other data that identifies the files.

a change log: the changes should be logged. To facilitate automatic processing of these files, the log entries must minimally specify a timestamp for the change, whether the change was a removal or an addition of files (we will address additions presently under the heading of conversions).

the next best version: In case of removal (or modification) of an CO, another version may be referenced, which comes as close to the modified CO as possible, in the optimal case only including legally required modifications, but if it is too costly to produce such a new adaptation of old COs, potentially also new additional data or corrections. For instance, in DeReKo, it may be that a certain year of a journal was first only included partially, but later was both cleared of illegal data and completed.

3.1. Delivering Signposts

We assume that delivery and processing of signposts are handled as outlined below. We would welcome a discussion of this approach.

In case an **unavailable CO** is retrieved, an HTTP 404 error is signalled, and signpost data is used to generate an error message that explains the situation and points the user to the next best version, if possible. As there are different use cases for the signpost, we suggest that besides delivering the signpost data or an error page as just described, the following convenience functions may be useful.

First, signposts may be used by human readers to access the CO. In this case a readable and human-friendly version of the information in the signpost may be presented. From there, access to the LO(s) will be possible. These will, however, under no circumstances be available via a persistent identifier, and there will be no guarantee that linking to them directly will have reliable result.

Secondly, a signpost may be used to automatically retrieve data. The focus of resource delivery should then be on machine-readability, namely as follows. If no additional requirements are signalled, the signpost file will be delivered, and an HTTP status of 300 *Multiple Choices* will be indicated, and a preferred choice will be signalled in the header. There is no long-term guarantee as to which format this will have, only that it is the format that, according to the expectations of the archive, suits the interest of a general user best. In case the user has an interest in retrieving specific file types, this may be signalled by asking for specific MIME types. If possible, the CO will be delivered in an object corresponding to the MIME type. If not, an HTTP 404 error will be signalled, and the signpost information will be used to generate a useful directions to get other realizations of the CO.

3.2. An Abstract Data Format for Signposts

In this section we present an abstract format for signposts. We also give a minimalist implementation of this format. We do not give an implementation in some existing format like CMDI, because this is a conceptual paper and we assume that the structure will be adapted after discussion in the community.

Remember that signposts are to be processed automatically as much as possible.

For a given CO, e.g. an audio recording or a transcription, the following is require (a simple XML grammar is provided at the end of the paper).

PID: the persistent identifier pointing to the CO, i.e. normally the URL of the signpost.

Pointers to LOs, e.g. to the audio file (or files of different formats) or to the transcription file (or the files of different formats), each pointer consisting of the following information:

- **State:** Every LO is either `"active"` or `"retired"`.
- **Creation and**, if applicable, **Retirement Dates:** It is thus reproducible what files were available at the time.
- **LO URL:** for retrieval
- **Format or MIME type:** to assure adequate processing
- **Information on the LOs:** like **size** or **check sums**

Log of Events in which the conceptual object was created and altered. This allows for reconstruction of availability and contributes to checking reproducibility.

- **Date** of the event.
- **Type of Change:** For conceptual objects, it can be seen when they were removed from the archive, and types of reasons are given using a closed vocabulary; we currently assume that creation, ingest, injunction and migration are sufficient.
- **Comment:** It is also possible to give more information in human-readable form.

Pointer to the Next Best Version For conceptual objects that are no longer available, a `<surrogate>` is presented which is only pointed at with a PID. This allows, theoretically, to chain signposts. While excessive use of this feature is not desirable, it is still a useful property in case injunctions are filed at greater temporal distance.

The first example points to a conceptual object like in the versioning example above. We assume we are in the year 2138. Let us assume that there are several metadata records pointing to our conceptual object, e.g. those of vc_4 and vc_5, as it may be part of different greater units. More importantly, the object was transcoded from the original MP4 Audio format to MP7 in 2028 and again, a hundred years later, to MP27. At the latter migration, the MP7 file was retired, as it is not the original and MP27 captures all significant properties of MP7 files. (The original MP4 file was kept, following the preservation policy of the IDS.) Programs that no longer can process the outdated MP4 audio can see that the object is available as MP27 as well and retrieve it. (As discussed above, implicit smartness can also be implemented.)

```
<?xml version="1.0" encoding="utf-8"?>
<signpost>
  <identity pid="http://PID-1"/>
  <logical-objects>
    <logical-object state="active"
      url="https://REPO/PATH/RECORDING-1"
      mime-type="application/mp4"
      creation-date="2021-07-07T02:00:00+02:00"
      byte-size="123456">
      <!-- check sum as element to allow different,
           non-hardcoded types -->
      <check-sum type="SHA-512" value="402550..."/>
    </logical-object>
    <logical-object
      url="https://REPO/PATH/RECORDING-1?format=mp7"
      mime-type="application/mp7"
      creation-date="2028-05-15T02:00:00+02:00"
      state="retired" retirement-date="2128-05-15
           T02:00:00+02:00"
      byte-size="23456">
      <check-sum type="SHA-512" value="31324..."/>
    </logical-object>
    <logical-object state="active"
      url="https://REPO/PATH/RECORDING-1?format=mp27"
      mime-type="application/mp27"
      creation-date="2128-05-15T02:00:00+02:00"
      byte-size="6789">
      <check-sum type="SHA-512" value="7a8b5a..."/>
    </logical-object>
  </logical-objects>
  <change-log>
    <entry date="2021-05-15T02:00:00+02:00"
      type="creation">File created</entry>
    <entry date="2021-07-07T02:00:00+02:00"
      type="ingest">File ingested into IDS LTA</entry>
    <entry date="2028-05-15T02:00:00+02:00"
      type="migration">converted to MP7</entry>
    <entry date="2128-05-15T02:00:00+02:00"
      type="migration">converted to MP27</entry>
  </change-log>
</signpost>
```

The second example may represent DeReKo data. Assume this is the 2020 volume of the *Postkutschenbote*. It was not yet completely digitized when it was ingested. Then an injunction was filed, making it necessary to remove the CO. For reasons of work economy, the reader is referred to a new edition (in the OAIS sense) of the work, which may already contain the full 2020 volume. As the CO as a whole is retired, all LOs have been, as well.

```
<?xml version="1.0" encoding="utf-8"?>
<signpost>
  <identity pid="http://PID-DEREKO-EXAMPLE-1-e1"/>
  <logical-objects>
    <logical-object url="https://REPO/PATH/NEWS-1"
      mime-type="application/tei+xml"
      creation-date="2021-07-07T13:37:23+02:00"
      state="retired"
      retirement-date="2021-08-08T13:37:23+12:05"
      byte-size="123456">
      <check-sum type="SHA-512" value="31324..."/>
    </logical-object>
  </logical-objects>
  <surrogate pid="http://PID-DEREKO-EXAMPLE-1-e2"
    type="edition">This version contains all original
         data except for the ones removed due to an
         injunction, and potentially more data.
  </surrogate>
  <change-log>
    <entry date="2021-01-01T13:37:23+02:00"
      type="creation">File created</entry>
    <entry date="2021-07-07T13:37:23+02:00"
      type="ingest">File ingested into IDS LTA</entry>
    <entry date="2021-08-08T13:37:23+12:05"
      type="injunction">File removed due to an
           injunction</entry>
  </change-log>
</signpost>
```

The third example concerns DeReKo data. Assume this is the 2019 volume of the *Mannheimer Spezielle Zeitung*. It was ingested, but an injunction was filed. As this hypothetical newspaper is one of the most-read in Germany and is particularly loved and used by corpus linguists for word usage statistics, a new version of this object was prepared, which is as close to the original data as possible. This should help maintain reproducibility as much as legally possible. On a terminological note, the surrogate does not constitute an OAIS version in this case, as the process is not the result of a migration. We still think that intuitive meaning of the term *version* comes closest to what we need here.

```
<?xml version="1.0" encoding="utf-8"?>
<signpost>
  <identity pid="http://PID-DEREKO-EXAMPLE-2-e1-v1"/>
  <logical-objects>
    <logical-object url="https://REPO/PATH/NEWS-2"
      mime-type="application/tei+xml"
      creation-date="2020-07-07T13:38:24+02:00"
      state="retired"
      retirement-date="2020-08-08T13:38:24+02:00"
      byte-size="123456">
      <check-sum type="SHA-512" value="31324..."/>
    </logical-object>
  </logical-objects>
  <surrogate pid="http://PID-DEREKO-EXAMPLE-2-e1-v2"
    type="version">This version contains all original
         data except for the ones removed due to an
         injunction.
  </surrogate>
  <change-log>
    <entry date="2020-01-01T13:38:24+01:00"
      type="creation">File created</entry>
    <entry date="2020-07-07T13:38:24+02:00"
      type="ingest">File ingested into IDS LTA</entry>
    <entry date="2020-08-08T13:38:24+02:00"
      type="injunction">File adapted due to an
           injunction</entry>
  </change-log>
</signpost>
```

4. Conclusion and Outlook

We assume that the concept of signpost is useful to address the problems of unavoidable data change in LTA, versioning

of growing corpora and data migration as sketched in this paper. We discussed theoretical points and illustrated the use of signposts with concrete, if partly fictional examples.
Some details of the proposal should be discussed further, for instance:
Does the signpost need something like a title or a short human-readable summary of the conceptual object's place in the corpus? We decided against this in the examples we presented, as it cannot trivially be generated automatically.
Is it necessary to keep the information on logical objects that have been removed, especially in the case the conceptual object is no longer available? An argument in favour is that this may help to ensure reproducibility; this would only be useful, though, if there were standardized procedures for citing logical objects that include, e.g., the file checksums used in the signpost.
How adequate is the assumption that a presentation layer complements the metadata? We suggested above that pointers to later versions of an object can be implemented in the presentation layer to avoid adjustment of metadata; however, this conflates data modelling and presentation and hence introduces new challenges to data repositories.
Moreover, it may be useful to implement the signpost format in a way more compatible with established metadata standards, for instance CMDI (Broeder et al., 2012), or to define the vocabulary in a formal way such as using Semantic Web technologies like RDF(S) (see, e.g., McBride, 2003).

5. Acknowledgements

We thank Thorsten Trippel (SFS, University of Tübingen) for insightful discussions on metadata.

A Simple SignpostML grammar

A simple RelaxNG (Clark and Murata, 2001) grammar (using compact syntax) is provided below. The documents above are valid against this grammar.

```
start = element signpost {
  element identity { attribute pid { xsd:anyURI } },
  (AliveObject | DeadObject),
  element change-log {
    element entry {
      attribute date { xsd:dateTime },
      attribute type {
        "creation" | "ingest" |
        "injunction" | "migration" },
      text
    }+
  }
}

AliveObject = element logical-objects {
  AliveLO, (DeadLO*, AliveLO*)*
}

DeadObject =
element logical-objects { DeadLO+ },
element surrogate {
  attribute pid { xsd:anyURI },
  attribute type { "edition" | "version" },
  text
} ?

LOParts = attribute url { xsd:anyURI },
  attribute creation-date { xsd:dateTime },
  attribute mime-type { text },
  attribute byte-size { xsd:integer },
  element check-sum {
    attribute type { "SHA-512" },
    attribute value { text } }+

DeadLOAttributes = attribute state { "retired" },
  attribute retirement-date { xsd:dateTime }?

AliveLOAttributes = attribute state { "active" }

DeadLO = element logical-object {
  DeadLOAttributes, LOParts }

AliveLO = element logical-object {
  AliveLOAttributes, LOParts }
```

6. Bibliographical References

Bański, P., Bingel, J., Diewald, N., Frick, E., Hanl, M., Kupietz, M., Pezik, P., Schnober, C., and Witt, A. (2013). KorAP: the new corpus analysis platform at IDS Mannheim. In Vetulani, Z. and Uszkoreit, H., editors, *Human Language Technologies as a Challenge for Computer Science and Linguistics. Proceedings of the 6th Language and Technology Conference*, Poznań. Fundacja Uniwersytetu im. A. Mickiewicza.

Bodmer, F. (2005). COSMAS II. Recherchieren in den Korpora des IDS. *Sprachreport*, 3/2005:2–5.

Bray, T., Paoli, J., and Sperberg-McQueen, C. M. (1997). Extensible markup language XML. W3C Recommendation TR-XML, The World Wide Web Consortium.

Broeder, D., Windhouwer, M., Van Uytvanck, D., Goosen, T., and Trippel, T. (2012). CMDI: a component metadata infrastructure. In *Describing LRs with metadata: towards flexibility and interoperability in the documentation of LR workshop programme*, volume 1.

Burnard, L. and Bauman, S., editors (2020). *Guidelines for Electronic Text Encoding and Interchange*. Text Encoding Initiative, Chicago, New York. version 1.0.0 2007; latest release 4.0.0 on 2020-02-13.

Caron, B., De La Houssaye, J., Ledoux, T., and Reecht, S. (2017). Life and death of an information package: Implementing the lifecycle in a multi-purpose preservation system. In *iPRES 2017 14th International Conference on Digital Preservation*, Kyōto, Japan.

CCSDS (2012). *Reference model for an open archival information system (OAIS)*. CCSDS, Washington, 2 edition.

Clark, J. and Murata, M., editors (2001). *RELAX NG Specification*. Organization for the Advancement of Structured Information Standards.

Conway, E., Giaretta, D., Lambert, S., and Matthews, B. (2011). Curating scientific research data for the long term: a preservation analysis method in context. *The International Journal of Digital Curation*, 6(2).

Deutsche Forschungsgemeinschaft (2015). Handreichung: Informationen zu rechtlichen Aspekten bei der Handhabung von Sprachkorpora. DFG-Leitlinien zum Umgang mit Forschungsdaten. http://www.dfg.de/foerderung/

antragstellung_begutachtung_entscheidung/antragstellende/antragstellung/nachnutzung_forschungsdaten/.

Digital Preservation Coalition (2015). *Digital Preservation Handbook*. Digital Preservation Coalition, 2 edition.

Fecher, B. and Friesike, S. (2014). Open science: one term, five schools of thought. In *Opening science*, pages 17–47. Springer.

ISO (2016). ISO 24624:2016 Language resource management – Transcription of spoken language. Technical report, ISO, Genève.

ISO8879:1986 (1986). Information processing – Text and Office Systems – Standard Generalized Markup Language (SGML). Standard No. ISO 8879:1986, International Organization for Standardization.

Kupietz, M., Belica, C., Keibel, H., and Witt, A. (2010). The German Reference Corpus DeReKo: A Primordial Sample for Linguistic Research. In Calzolari, N., Choukri, K., Maegaard, B., Mariani, J., Odjik, J., Piperidis, S., Rosner, M., and Tapias, D., editors, *Proceedings of the Seventh conference on International Language Resources and Evaluation (LREC'10)*, pages 1848–1854, Valletta/Paris. European Language Resources Association (ELRA). http://www.lrec-conf.org/proceedings/lrec2010/pdf/414_Paper.pdf.

Kupietz, M., Lüngen, H., Bański, P., and Belica, C. (2014). Maximizing the potential of very large corpora: 50 years of big language data at IDS Mannheim. In Kupietz, M., Biber, H., Lüngen, H., Bański, P., Breiteneder, E., Mörth, K., Witt, A., and Takhsha, J., editors, *Proceedings of the LREC 2014 Workshop "Challenges in the Management of Large Corpora" (CMLC-2)*, pages 1–6, Reykjavik/Paris. European Language Resources Association (ELRA). http://nbn-resolving.de/urn:nbn:de:bsz:mh39-31634.

Kupietz, M., Lüngen, H., Kamocki, P., and Witt, A. (2018). The German Reference Corpus DeReKo: New Developments – New Opportunities. In Calzolari, N., Choukri, K., Cieri, C., Declerck, T., Goggi, S., Hasida, K., Isahara, H., Maegaard, B., Mariani, J., Mazo, H., Moreno, A., Odijk, J., Piperidis, S., and Tokunaga, T., editors, *Proceedings of the Eleventh International Conference on Language Resources and Evaluation (LREC'18)*, pages 4353–4360, Miyazaki/Paris. European Language Resources Association (ELRA). http://www.lrec-conf.org/proceedings/lrec2018/pdf/737.pdf.

Lehr, U. and Thomae, H., editors (1987). *Formen seelischen Alterns*. Enke, Stuttgart.

Lüngen, H. and Sperberg-McQueen, C. M. (2012). A TEI P5 Document Grammar for the IDS Text Model. *Journal of the Text Encoding Initiative*, 3:1–18. http://jtei.revues.org/508.

McBride, B. (2003). The resource description framework (RDF) and its vocabulary description language RDFS. In Stab, S. and Studer, R., editors, *Handbook of Ontologies*, chapter 3, pages 29–50. Springer, Berlin, Heidelberg, New York.

Neuroth, H., Oßwald, A., Scheffel, R., Strathmann, S., and Jehn, M., editors (2009). *nestor Handbuch : eine kleine Enzyklopädie der digitalen Langzeitarchivierung*. nestor, version 2.0 [3/2010] edition.

Schmidt, T. (2016). Construction and dissemination of a corpus of spoken interaction – tools and workflows in the FOLK project. *Journal for Language Technology and Computational Linguistics (JLCL)*, 31(1):127–154.

Schmidt, T. (2017). DGD – die Datenbank für Gesprochenes Deutsch. Mündliche Korpora am Institut für Deutsche Sprache (IDS) in Mannheim. *Zeitschrift für germanistische Linguistik*, 45(3):451–463.

Schmidt, T. and Wörner, K. (2014). Exmaralda. In Durand, J., Gut, U., and Kristoffersen, G., editors, *The Oxford handbook of corpus phonology*. Oxford University Press, Oxford.

Sperberg-McQueen, C. M. and Burnard, L., editors (1999). *Guidelines for Electronic Text Encoding and Interchange*. Text Encoding Initiative, Chicago, New York. initial release 1994-05-16; last version dated May 1999.

Teubert, W. and Belica, C. (2014). Von der Linguistischen Datenverarbeitung am IDS zur Mannheimer Schule der Korpuslinguistik. In Steinle, M. and Berens, F. J., editors, *Ansichten und Einsichten. 50 Jahre Institut für Deutsche Sprache*, pages 320–328. Institut für Deutsche Sprache, Mannheim.

Wildgans, J., Weitzmann, J., and Ketzan, E. (2017). Guidelines for building language corpora under German Law – by the DFG Review Board on Linguistics. https://www.dfg.de/download/pdf/foerderung/antragstellung/forschungsdaten/guidelines_review_board_linguistics_corpora.pdf.

Wilkinson, M. D., Dumontier, M., Aalbersberg, I. J., Appleton, G., Axton, M., Baak, A., Blomberg, N., Boiten, J.-W., da Silva Santos, L. B., Bourne, P. E., et al. (2016). The FAIR guiding principles for scientific data management and stewardship. *Scientific data*, 3.

7. Language Resource References

Leibniz-Institut für Deutsche Sprache (2020). German Reference Corpus DeReKo. Deutsches Referenzkorpus, DeReKo-2020-I. PID: http://hdl.handle.net/10932/00-04B6-B898-AD1A-8101-4.

Schmidt, T. and Gasch, J. (2019). Datenbank für Gesprochenes Deutsch (DGD). Leibniz-Institut für Deutsche Sprache, 2.13. https://dgd.ids-mannheim.de.

Proceedings of he 8th Workshop on Challenges in the Management of Large Corpora, pages 10–14
Language Resources and Evaluation Conference (LREC 2020), Marseille, 11–16 May 2020

Evaluating a Dependency Parser on DeReKo

Peter Fankhauser, Bich-Ngoc Do, Marc Kupietz
IDS Mannheim, Heidelberg University, IDS Mannheim
Germany, Germany, Germany
fankhauser@ids-mannheim.de, do@cl.uni-heidelberg.de, kupietz@ids-mannheim.de

Abstract

We evaluate a graph-based dependency parser on DeReKo, a large corpus of contemporary German. The dependency parser is trained on the German dataset from the SPMRL 2014 Shared Task which contains text from the news domain, whereas DeReKo also covers other domains including fiction, science, and technology. To avoid the need for costly manual annotation of the corpus, we use the parser's probability estimates for unlabeled and labeled attachment as main evaluation criterion. We show that these probability estimates are highly correlated with the actual attachment scores on a manually annotated test set. On this basis, we compare estimated parsing scores for the individual domains in DeReKo, and show that the scores decrease with increasing distance of a domain to the training corpus.

Keywords: Dependency Parsing, Large Corpora, Evaluation

1. Background and Aims

The Leibniz Institute for the German Language (IDS) has been building up the German Reference Corpus DeReKo (Kupietz et al., 2010) since its foundation in the mid-1960s and maintains it continuously. Since 2004, two new releases per year have been published. These are made available to the German linguistic community via the corpus analysis platforms COSMAS II (Bodmer, 2005) and KorAP (Bański et al., 2013), which allows the query and display of dependency annotations. DeReKo covers a broad spectrum of topics and text types (Kupietz et al., 2018). The latest release DeReKo 2020-I (Leibniz-Institut für Deutsche Sprache, 2020) contains 46.9 billion words. The number of registered users is about 45,000.

Linguistic Annotations in DeReKo DeReKo also features many linguistic annotation layers, including 4 different morphosyntactic annotations as well as one constituency and dependency annotation. The only dependency annotation is currently provided by the Maltparser (Nivre et al., 2006), however, based on a different dependency scheme. One of DeReKo's design principles is to distinguish between observations and interpretations. Accordingly (automatic) linguistic annotations are systematically handled as theory-dependent and potentially error-prone *interpretations*. DeReKo's approach to make them usable for linguistic applications is to offer several alternatives, ideally independent annotations (Belica et al., 2011) on all levels. With KorAP, users can then use the degree of agreement between alternative annotations to get an idea of the accuracy they can expect for specific queries and query combinations. By using disjunctive or conjunctive queries on annotation alternatives, users can, in addition, try to maximise recall or precision, respectively (Kupietz et al., 2017). With this approach, the direct comparison of the average accuracy of two annotation tools or models does not play a decisive role, since normally one would add both variants anyway. However, since DeReKo is first of all very large and secondly permanently extended and improved, it is a prerequisite that an annotation tool is sufficiently performant to be applicable to DeReKo or to additional corpus text within reasonable time. This is not always the case, especially with syntactic annotations.

Given this background, the evaluation criteria for dependency annotations might differ from those in other applications. Important factors are above all: 1) sufficient performance and stability of the annotation tool; 2) independence from existing annotations; 3) at least selective improvements over existing annotations 4) Adaptability to domains outside the training data

2. Parser and Corpora

Parser The evaluated parser is a re-implementation of the graph-based dependency parser from Dozat and Manning (2017). The parser employs several layers of bidirectional Long Short-Term Memory (LSTM) (Hochreiter and Schmidhuber, 1997) units to encode the words in a sentence. These representations are then used to train two biaffine classifiers, one to predict the head of a word and the other to predict the dependency label between two words. At prediction time, the dependency head and label for each word is selected as the word and label with the highest estimates given by the classifiers. The parser is available on Github (Do, 2019).

Training data We train the parser on the German dataset of the SPMRL 2014 Shared Task (Seddah et al., 2014) with the hyperparameters recommended by the authors. The dataset contains 40,000 sentences (760000 tokens) in the training set and 5,000 sentences (81700, 97000 tokens) for both development and testing. We use the predicted POS tags provided by the shared task organizers. For some evaluations we also use external word embeddings (see Section 3.) trained on DeReKo.

Evaluation data As evaluation data we use a sample of release 2019-I (Leibniz-Institut für Deutsche Sprache, 2019) of the German Reference Corpus DeReKo with 3670 Mio tokens from 11 domains. For a breakdown see Table 3. The corpus has been tokenized and part-of-speech tagged by the treetagger (Schmid, 1994). Parsing the corpus on a TESLA P4 GPU (8 GB) takes about 100 hours. For comparison, parsing with Malt 1.9.2 (liblinear) takes 34 wall-clock hours (38 CPU-hours) on the same machine equipped with enough

RAM and Intel Xeon Gold 6148 CPUs (at 2.40 GHz), when the corpus is processed sequentially.
This means that parsing with the malt parser is much more performant, especially since it can be distributed more easily to several existing computers and cores. On the other hand, parsing with the biaffine LSTM parser is at least sufficiently performant in the case of DeReKo. By using an additional GPU, DeReKo could be parsed within less than 4 weeks.

3. Overall Accuracy

As basic measures for parsing accuracy we use unlabeled and labeled attachment scores, UAS and LAS. UAS gives the percentage of dependency relations with the correct head and dependent, and LAS the percentage of correctly attached and labelled dependencies. In addition, we also look at the attachment estimates given by the two biaffine classifiers of the parser (see Equations 2 and 3 in Dozat and Manning (2017)). The estimates for the head of a dependency (unlabeled attachment estimate, UAE) and for its label (independent labeled attachment estimate, ILAE) are independent. Thus we calculate the labeled attachment estimate LAE as the product of UAE and ILAE.

External Word Embeddings Table 1 compares the attachment scores and estimates for different embeddings on the test set. For SPMRL embeddings we have experimented with embedding dimensions 100 and 200, for DEREKO embeddings we have used 200 dimensions throughout. The internal SPMRL embeddings are trained as part of the parser training process, the DEREKO embeddings have been trained using the structured skip gram approach introduced in (Ling et al., 2015) on the complete DeReKo-2017-I corpus (Institut für Deutsche Sprache, 2017) consisting of over 30 billion tokens. DEREKO1 uses the embeddings for the most frequent 100.000 words, DEREKO2 and DEREKO5 the most frequent 200.000 and most frequent 500.000 words respectively. The best overall scores are achieved with DEREKO2 leading to an improvement of about 0.5% in UAS and 0.8% in LAS w.r.t. the baseline of SPMRL without external embeddings. Taking into account a larger vocabulary (DEREKO5) does not improve the scores, nor does concatenating the internal embeddings of the parser with the DEREKO embeddings DRK2+SPMRL.

Scores vs. Estimates Comparing the scores with the parsers' estimates along varying embeddings also shows that they are highly correlated with the spearman rank correlation coefficient $\rho = 0.89$ between UAS and UAE, and $\rho = 0.94$ between LAS and LAE.

embeddings	dim	UAS	LAS	UAE	LAE
SPMRL	100	93.99	92.33	95.84	94.11
SPMRL	200	94.15	92.59	96.23	94.66
DEREKO1	200	94.30	93.00	97.08	95.90
DEREKO2	200	**94.51**	**93.16**	**97.10**	**95.94**
DEREKO5	200	93.98	92.50	95.88	94.40
DRK2+SPMRL	200	94.02	92.58	96.97	95.79

Table 1: Attachment scores and estimates for different word embeddings

All further evaluations use the model with the best scores DEREKO2.
Figure 1 plots the attachment scores against the attachment estimates between 75% and 100% in bins of 1%, i.e., the value at 99% estimate is the average score of all attachments with an estimate between 99% and 100%, and so on, and estimates smaller than 75% are bundled together with an average score of about 50%. Blue boxes stand for UAS and red circles for the LAS. Also from this perspective, the estimates strongly correlate with the scores. However, the estimates are typically overly confident. For the about 70% (63%) of attachments with an unlabeled (labeled) estimate $\geq$ 99% we get 99.79% UAS and 99.84% LAS. For the about 15% attachments with estimates between 98% and 99%, UAS and LAS are at about 96%. For lower estimates the difference between estimate and actual score increases. Nevertheless, the estimates predict the actual scores rather well, with Spearman's $\rho = 0.94$ for UAE vs. UAS, and $\rho = 0.99$ for LAE vs. LAS.

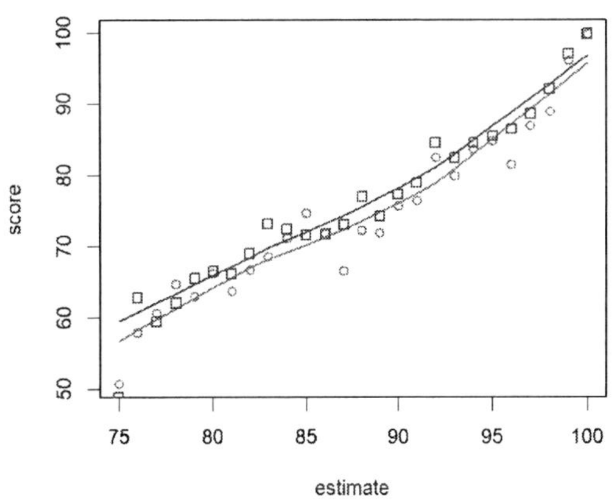

Figure 1: Attachment Estimates vs. Scores

4. Breakdown by Dependency Label

Table 2 breaks down scores and estimates by dependency label[1]. PROB gives the relative frequency of a dependency label in percent, UERR gives the percentage of overall error for unlabeled attachment, LERR the percentage for labeled attachment, REC the recall and PREC the precision for labeled attachment only, not taking into account the correctness of head and dependent.
In terms of individual scores, relatively rare dependencies such as Parataxes or Appositions perform worst. However, the frequency PROB of dependencies does not seem to have a strong influence on score, $\rho = -0.05$ for UAS vs. PROB, and $\rho = 0.42$ for LAS vs. PROB.
In terms of contribution to the overall error, Modifier (MO), Modifier of NP to the right (MNR), and Punctuation (X..) account for more than 50%. MO is often mislabelled as MNR or Object Preposition (OP) and vice versa, which typically also assigns the head incorrectly, as evident by the

[1]The SPMRL 2014 Shared Task for German uses the dependency scheme adopted by Seeker and Kuhn (2012)

rather low UAS of 88%. Punctuation is virtually never confused with other labels, its score of 91% is almost exclusively due to incorrect head or dependent attachments.

In terms of recall, rare dependencies such as Vocative (VO), Reported Speech (RS), and Object Genitive (OG) stand out, e.g. only 1 out of 15 occurrences of Vocative is correctly labeled, and less than half of RS and OG. Also, rare dependencies tend to depict low precision.

Comparing scores with estimates broken down by dependency label again reveals a rather strong correlation of $\rho = 0.89$ for unlabeled and $\rho = 0.75$ for labeled attachments.

5. Domain Dependence

Having established attachment estimates as a fairly reliable predictor for attachment scores, we can derive estimates for DEREKO for which we do not have any test data.

Table 3 breaks down estimates by domain, sorted by UAE. It can be seen that domains that are close to the news domain, for which the parser has been trained, such as politics, finance, and health achieve the best overall estimates. In contrast, domains, such as fiction, culture, and sports depict significantly lower estimates.

domain	UAE	LAE	JS_dep	JS_pos	Mio tokens
politics	95.85	95.14	0.13	0.24	820
finance	95.75	95.05	0.20	0.54	219
health	95.74	94.98	0.18	0.47	66
science	95.56	94.81	0.18	0.44	140
society	95.34	94.66	0.40	0.68	841
technology	95.18	94.50	0.15	0.45	196
leisure	95.15	94.43	0.24	0.32	469
nature	95.04	94.33	0.57	0.87	0.17
culture	94.52	93.79	0.41	0.31	453
sports	94.12	93.59	0.60	0.77	464
fiction	92.66	92.16	2.03	2.47	0.43

Table 3: Attachment estimates by domain

One way to measure the distance between domains w.r.t. to dependencies is to compare their distributions over dependency labels. JS_dep gives the Jensen-Shannon Divergence ($*100$) between the dependency distributions of the individual domains in DEREKO and the SPMRL training corpus. The closest is politics, and the most distant is fiction. Indeed, we can observe a strong negative correlation between UAE and JS_dep of -0.92 (Pearson) and LAE and JS_dep of -0.84. These findings are corroborated by the likewise fairly strong negative correlations between attachment estimates and JS_pos the JS divergence measured on the part-of-speech distributions; -0.48 for UAE and -0.84 for LAE.

6. Summary

We have presented an evaluation of a graph-based dependency parser on a large corpus of contemporary German for which no manually labelled test set is available. To this end, we have analyzed the correlation between actual attachment scores measured on the SPMRL test set with the parser's attachment estimates, and shown that they are highly correlated along variations in pretrained word embeddings (Table 1), as well as along the different kinds of dependencies (Table 2). On this basis, we have shown that the parser's attachment estimates are consistently domain dependent, with estimates varying up to 3% depending on distance of the domain to the training set. This suggests that it may be fruitful to experiment with domain adaptation techniques such as (Yu et al., 2015) in order to improve scores. For future work, we plan to systematically compare scores and estimates with the Malt parser. Depending on the results, we plan to apply the parser to the entire DeReKo in one of the upcoming releases and make the new dependency annotation layer available to German linguistics for research and analysis via KorAP.

7. Bibliographical References

Bański, P., Bingel, J., Diewald, N., Frick, E., Hanl, M., Kupietz, M., Pezik, P., Schnober, C., and Witt, A. (2013). KorAP: the new corpus analysis platform at IDS Mannheim. In Vetulani, Z. and Uszkoreit, H., editors, *Human Language Technologies as a Challenge for Computer Science and Linguistics. Proceedings of the 6th Language and Technology Conference*, Poznań. Fundacja Uniwersytetu im. A. Mickiewicza.

Belica, C., Kupietz, M., Lüngen, H., and Witt, A. (2011). The morphosyntactic annotation of DEREKO: Interpretation, opportunities and pitfalls. In Konopka, M., Kubczak, J., Mair, C., Šticha, F., and Wassner, U., editors, *Selected contributions from the conference Grammar and Corpora 2009*, pages 451–471, Tübingen. Gunter Narr Verlag.

Bodmer, F. (2005). COSMAS II. Recherchieren in den Korpora des IDS. *Sprachreport*, 3/2005:2–5.

Do, B.-N. (2019). Theano biaffine dependency parser. https://github.com/bichngocdo/theano-biaffine-parser. Accessed 2020-02-20.

Dozat, T. and Manning, C. D. (2017). Deep biaffine attention for neural dependency parsing. In *5th International Conference on Learning Representations, ICLR 2017, Toulon, France, April 24-26, 2017, Conference Track Proceedings*. OpenReview.net.

Hochreiter, S. and Schmidhuber, J. (1997). Long short-term memory. *Neural Computation*, 9(8):1735–1780.

Kupietz, M., Belica, C., Keibel, H., and Witt, A. (2010). The German Reference Corpus DEREKO: A Primordial Sample for Linguistic Research. In Calzolari, N., Choukri, K., Maegaard, B., Mariani, J., Odjik, J., Piperidis, S., Rosner, M., and Tapias, D., editors, *Proceedings of the Seventh conference on International Language Resources and Evaluation (LREC'10)*, pages 1848–1854, Valletta/Paris. European Language Resources Association (ELRA). http://www.lrec-conf.org/proceedings/lrec2010/pdf/414_Paper.pdf.

Kupietz, M., Diewald, N., Hanl, M., and Margaretha, E. (2017). Möglichkeiten der Erforschung grammatischer Variation mithilfe von KorAP. In Konopka, M. and Wöllstein, A., editors, *Grammatische Variation. Empirische Zugänge und theoretische Modellierung*, pages 319–329.

lb	meaning	UAS	LAS	UAE	LAE	PROB	UERR	LERR	REC	PREC
AC	Adpositional Case Marker	95.38	95.38	99.16	99.10	0.14	0.12	0.09	99.21	96.92
ADC	Adjective Component	100.00	75.00	100.00	100.00	0.00	0.00	0.00	75.00	75.00
AG	Attribute Genitive	97.96	97.25	97.85	97.08	2.45	0.91	0.99	98.62	98.18
AMS	Measure Argument of Adjective	95.12	89.02	95.36	92.52	0.09	0.08	0.14	97.33	89.02
APP	Apposition	78.64	67.73	85.92	74.18	0.48	1.87	2.27	71.58	75.00
AVC	Adverbial Phrase Component	66.67	66.67	65.50	64.91	0.00	0.00	0.00	50.00	66.67
CC	Comparative Complement	84.74	84.34	89.17	87.25	0.27	0.75	0.62	93.28	89.16
CD	Coordinating Conjunction	93.08	92.99	95.33	95.24	2.43	3.06	2.49	99.82	99.42
CJ	Conjunct	91.10	89.64	94.33	92.48	3.72	6.03	5.64	91.56	92.09
CM	Comparative Conjunction	97.97	97.97	97.65	97.65	0.32	0.12	0.10	99.33	100.00
CP	Complementizer	99.24	99.24	99.52	99.48	0.86	0.12	0.10	100.00	100.00
CVC	Collocational Verb Construction	98.70	77.92	99.23	86.23	0.08	0.02	0.26	84.51	77.92
DA	Dative	94.95	90.09	95.68	88.33	0.58	0.53	0.84	87.50	92.90
DM	Discourse Marker	80.00	73.33	88.50	84.04	0.02	0.07	0.08	66.67	80.00
EP	Expletive	100.00	88.60	99.42	87.96	0.21	0.00	0.35	91.94	88.60
JU	Junctor	89.95	89.95	96.12	95.64	0.24	0.44	0.35	95.18	99.09
MNR	Modifier of Np to the right	78.77	75.20	84.97	81.05	2.84	10.98	10.30	84.03	82.25
MO	Modifier	88.46	86.65	90.60	87.81	13.01	27.35	25.40	93.73	94.75
NG	Negation	82.43	82.43	89.44	89.43	0.56	1.79	1.44	99.81	99.03
NK	Noun Kernerl Modifier	99.29	99.14	99.53	99.27	30.32	3.92	3.81	99.46	99.48
NMC	Numerical Component	99.69	98.75	99.61	99.15	0.35	0.02	0.06	98.75	98.75
OA	Object Accusative	97.00	92.74	97.01	92.56	3.55	1.94	3.77	96.11	93.69
OC	Object Clausal	97.83	95.11	97.97	95.80	4.00	1.58	2.86	96.71	95.93
OG	Object Genitive	100.00	71.43	90.93	76.07	0.02	0.00	0.08	47.62	71.43
OP	Object Preposition	95.85	72.89	96.21	75.99	0.73	0.55	2.89	76.47	73.19
PAR	Parataxis	62.20	50.40	76.51	62.22	0.41	2.82	2.97	56.64	65.15
PD	Predicative	98.05	90.33	98.24	90.21	1.11	0.39	1.57	88.90	90.72
PG	Pseudo Genitive	94.13	89.87	94.51	87.18	0.41	0.44	0.61	89.43	92.53
PH	Placeholder	100.00	86.21	99.70	73.44	0.03	0.00	0.06	83.33	86.21
PM	Morphological Particle	100.00	100.00	100.00	100.00	0.47	0.00	0.00	99.77	100.00
PNC	Proper Noun Component	96.16	95.04	97.73	96.44	1.36	0.95	0.99	95.91	95.60
RC	Relative Clause	83.48	82.84	88.61	88.08	0.84	2.53	2.11	98.82	97.55
RE	Repeated Element	87.86	87.50	93.34	91.54	0.30	0.66	0.55	91.79	87.86
RS	Reported Speech	85.19	55.56	88.35	73.58	0.03	0.08	0.20	42.86	55.56
RT	Root	94.97	94.97	98.66	98.29	5.94	5.44	4.37	97.35	94.97
SB	Subject	98.53	96.99	98.72	96.58	7.18	1.92	3.16	96.79	97.20
SBP	Subject Passivized	92.66	81.36	95.09	84.73	0.19	0.25	0.52	92.31	81.36
SVP	Separable Verb Prefix	99.40	99.00	99.36	99.23	0.54	0.06	0.08	99.80	99.60
UC	(Idiosyncratic) unit component	74.19	69.89	87.14	85.83	0.10	0.47	0.44	84.44	81.72
VO	Vocative	100.00	100.00	98.33	66.42	0.00	0.00	0.00	6.67	100.00
X..	Other (Punctuation)	91.36	91.36	95.04	95.04	13.80	21.72	17.44	99.30	99.76

Table 2: Scores and Estimates by Dependency Label

De Gruyter, Berlin. http://nbn-resolving.de/urn:nbn:de:bsz:mh39-59681.

Kupietz, M., Lüngen, H., Kamocki, P., and Witt, A. (2018). The German Reference Corpus DeReKo: New Developments – New Opportunities. In Calzolari, N., Choukri, K., Cieri, C., Declerck, T., Goggi, S., Hasida, K., Isahara, H., Maegaard, B., Mariani, J., Mazo, H., Moreno, A., Odijk, J., Piperidis, S., and Tokunaga, T., editors, *Proceedings of the Eleventh International Conference on Language Resources and Evaluation (LREC'18)*, pages 4353–4360, Miyazaki/Paris. European Language Resources Association (ELRA). http://www.lrec-conf.org/proceedings/lrec2018/pdf/737.pdf.

Ling, W., Dyer, C., Black, A., and Trancoso, I. (2015). Two/too simple adaptations of word2vec for syntax problems. In *Proceedings of the 2015 Conference of the North American Chapter of the Association for Computational Linguistics – Human Language Technologies (NAACL HLT 2015)*, pages 1299—1304, Denver, CO.

Nivre, J., Hall, J., and Nilsson, J. (2006). Maltparser: A data-driven parser-generator for dependency parsing. In *LREC*, volume 6, pages 2216–2219.

Schmid, H. (1994). Probabilistic part-of-speech tagging using decision trees. In *International Conference on New Methods in Language Processing*, pages 44–49, Manchester, UK. https://www.cis.uni-muenchen.de/~schmid/tools/TreeTagger/data/tree-tagger1.pdf.

Seddah, D., Kübler, S., and Tsarfaty, R. (2014). Introducing the SPMRL 2014 shared task on parsing morphologically-rich languages. In *Proceedings of the First Joint Workshop on Statistical Parsing of Morphologically Rich Languages and Syntactic Analysis of Non-Canonical Languages*, pages 103–109, Dublin, Ireland. Dublin City University.

Seeker, W. and Kuhn, J. (2012). Making ellipses explicit in dependency conversion for a German treebank. In *Proceedings of the Eighth International Conference on Language Resources and Evaluation (LREC'12)*, pages 3132–3139, Istanbul, Turkey. European Language Resources Association (ELRA).

Yu, J., Elkaref, M., and Bohnet, B. (2015). Domain adaptation for dependency parsing via self-training. In *Proceedings of the 14th International Conference on Parsing Technologies*, pages 1–10, Bilbao, Spain. Association for Computational Linguistics.

8. Language Resource References

Institut für Deutsche Sprache (2017). German Reference Corpus DeReKo-2017-I. PID: http://hdl.handle.net/10932/00-0373-23CD-C58F-FF01-3.

Leibniz-Institut für Deutsche Sprache (2019). German Reference Corpus DeReKo-2019-I. PID: http://hdl.handle.net/10932/00-04BB-AF28-4A4A-2801-5.

Leibniz-Institut für Deutsche Sprache (2020). German Reference Corpus DeReKo-2020-I. PID: http://hdl.handle.net/10932/00-04B6-B898-AD1A-8101-4.

Proceedings of he 8th Workshop on Challenges in the Management of Large Corpora, pages 15–23
Language Resources and Evaluation Conference (LREC 2020), Marseille, 11–16 May 2020

French Contextualized Word-Embeddings with a sip of CaBeRnet: a New French Balanced Reference Corpus

Murielle Popa-Fabre[1,2], Pedro Javier Ortiz Suárez[1,3], Benoît Sagot[1], Eric de la Clergerie[1]
[1]ALMAnaCH - Inria, [2]LLF - Université de Paris, [3]Sorbonne Université
2 rue Simone Iff, 75012 Paris, France
{murielle.fabre, pedro.ortiz, benoit.sagot, Eric.De_La_Clergerie}@inria.fr

Abstract

This paper investigates the impact of different types and size of training corpora on language models. By asking the fundamental question of quality versus quantity, we compare four French corpora by pre-training four different ELMos and evaluating them on dependency parsing, POS-tagging and Named Entities Recognition downstream tasks. We present and asses the relevance of a new balanced French corpus, CaBeRnet, that features a representative range of language usage, including a balanced variety of genres (oral transcriptions, newspapers, popular magazines, technical reports, fiction, academic texts), in oral and written styles. We hypothesize that a linguistically representative corpus will allow the language models to be more efficient, and therefore yield better evaluation scores on different evaluation sets and tasks.

Keywords: Balanced French Corpus, Language Models, French, BERT, ELMo, Tagging, Parsing, NER

1. Introduction

The question of quality versus size of training corpora is increasingly gaining attention and interest in the context of the latest developments in neural language models' performance. The longstanding issue of corpora "representativeness" is here addressed, in order to grasp to what extent a linguistically balanced cross-genre language sample is sufficient for a language model to gain in accuracy for contextualized word-embeddings on different NLP tasks.

Several increasingly larger corpora are nowadays compiled from the web, i.e. frWAC (Baroni et al., 2009), CCNet (Wenzek et al., 2019) and OSCAR-fr (Ortiz Suárez et al., 2019). However, does large size necessarily go along with better performance for language model training? Their alleged lack of representativeness has called for inventive ways of building a French balanced corpus offering new insights into language variation and NLP.

Following Biber's definition, "representativeness refers to the extent to which a sample includes the full range of variability in a population" (Biber, 1993, 244). We adopt a balanced approach by sampling a wide spectrum of language use and its cross-genre variability, be it situational (e.g. format, author, addressee, purposes, settings or topics) or linguistic, e.g. linked to distributional parameters like frequencies of word classes and genres. In this way, we developed two newly built corpora. The French Balanced Reference Corpus - *CaBeRnet* - includes a wide-ranging and balanced coverage of cross-genre language use to be maximally representative of French language and therefore yield good generalizations from. The second corpus, the *French Children Book Test* (CBT-fr), includes both narrative material and oral language use as present in youth literature, and will be used for domain-specific language model training. Both are inspired by existing American and English corpora, respectively COCA, the balanced Corpus of Contemporary American English (Davies, 2008), and the Children Book Test (Hill et al., 2015, CBT).

The second main contribution of this paper lies in the evaluation of the quality of the word-embeddings obtained by pre-training and fine-tuning on different corpora, that are made here publicly available. Based on the underlying assumption that a linguistically representative corpus would possibly generate better word-embeddings. We provide an evaluation-based investigation of how a balanced cross-genre corpus can yield improvements in the performance of neural language models like ELMo (Peters et al., 2018) on various downstream tasks. The two corpora, CaBeRnet and CBT-fr, and the ELMos will be distributed freely under Creative Commons License.

Specifically, we want to investigate the contribution of oral language use as present in different corpora. Through a series of comparisons, we contrast a more domain-specific and written corpus like Wikipedia-fr with the newly built domain-specific CBT-fr corpus which additionally features oral style dialogues, like the ones one can find in youth literature. To test for the effect of corpus size, we further compare a wide ranging corpora characterized by a variety of linguistic phenomena crawled from internet, like OSCAR (Ortiz Suárez et al., 2019), with our newly built French Balanced Reference Corpus CaBeRnet. Our aim is assess the benefits that can be gained from a balanced, multi-domain corpus such as CaBeRnet, despite its being 34 times smaller than the web-based OSCAR.

The paper is organized as follows. Sections 2. and 3. are dedicated to a descriptive overlook of the building of our two newly brewed corpora CaBeRnet and CBT-fr, including quantitative measures like type-token ratio and morphological richness. Section 4. presents the evaluation methods for POS-tagging, NER and dependency Parsing tasks, while results are introduced in §5. Finally, we conclude in §6. on the computational relevance of word-embeddings obtained through a balanced and representative corpus, and broaden the discussion on the benefits of smaller and noiseless corpora in neural NLP.

2. Corpora Building

2.1. CaBeRnet

CaBeRnet corpus was inspired by the genre partition of the American balanced corpus COCA, which currently contains over 618 million words of text (20 million words each year 1990-2019) and is equally divided among spoken, fiction, popular magazines, newspapers, and academic texts (Davies, 2008). A second reference, guiding our approach and sampling method, is one of the earliest precursors of balanced reference corpora: the BNC (Burnard, 2007), first covered a wide variety of genres, with the intention to be a representative sample of spoken and written language.

CaBeRnet was obtained by compiling existing data-sets and web-text extracted from different sources as detailed in this section. As shown in Table 1, genres sources are evenly divided (~120 million words each) into spoken, fiction, magazine, newspaper, academic to achieve genre-balanced between oral and written modality in newspapers or popular written style, technical reports and Wikipedia entries, fiction, literature or academic production).

CaBeRnet Oral The oral sub-portion gathers both oral transcriptions (ORFEO and Rhapsodie[1]) and Films subtitles (Open Subtitles.org), pruned from diacritics, interlocutors tagging and time stamps. To these transcriptions, the French European Parliament Proceedings (1996-2011), as presented in Koehn (2005), contributed a sample of more complex oral style with longer sentences and richer vocabulary.

CaBeRnet Popular Press The whole sub-portion of Popular Press is gathered from an open data-set from the *Est Républicain* (1999, 2002 and 2003), a regional press format[2]. It was selected to match popular style as it is characterized by easy-to-read press style and a wide range of every-day topics characterizing local regional press.

CaBeRnet Fiction & Literature The Fiction & Literature sub-portion was compiled from march 2019's Wiki Source and WikiBooks dump and extracted using WikiExtractor.py, a script that extracts and cleans text from a WikiMedia database dumps, by performing template expansion and preprocessing of template definitions.[3]

CaBeRnet News The News sub-portion builds upon web crawled elements, including Wikimedia's NewsComments and WikiNews reports from may 2019 WikiMedia dump, collected with a custom version of WikiExtractor.py. Newspaper's content gathered by the Chambers-Rostand Corpus (i.e. Le Monde 2002-2003, La Dépèche 2002-2003, L'Humanité 2002-2003) and *Le Monde diplomatique* opensource corpus were assembled to represent a higher register of written news style from different political and thematic horizons. Several months of French Press Agency reports (AFP, 2007-2011-2012) competed with more simple and telegraphic style the newspaper written sample of the corpus.[4]

CaBeRnet Academic The academic genre was also built from different sources including technical and educational texts from WikiBooks and Wikipedia dump (prior to 2016) for their thematic variety of highly specialized written production. ORFEO Corpus offered a small sample of academic writings like PHD dissertations and scientific articles encompassing a wide choice of disciplinary topics, and TALN Corpus[5] was included to represent more concise written style characterizing scientific abstracts and proceedings.

CaBeRnet Sub-set	Tokens	Unique Forms	TTR
Oral	122 864 888	291 744	0.0024
Popular	131 444 017	458 521	0.0035
News	132 708 943	462 971	0.0035
Fiction	198 343 802	983 195	0.0050
Academic	126 431 211	1 433 663	0.0113
Total	711 792 861	2 558 513	0.0036

Table 1: Comparison of number of unique forms in the different genres represented by CaBeRnet partition. TTR: Type-Token Ration. Lemmatization and tokenization was performed as described in §3..

For all sub-portions of CaBeRnet, visual inspection was performed to remove section titles, redundant meta-information linked to publishing schemes of each of the six news editor includes. This was manually achieved by compiling a rich set of regular expressions specific of each textual source to obtain clean plain text as an outcome.

2.2. French Children Book Test (CBT-fr)

The French Children Book Test (CBT-fr) was built upon its original English version, the Children Book Test (CBT) Hill et al. (2015)[6], which consists of books freely available on `www.gutenberg.org`Project Gutenberg.

Using youth literature and children books guarantees a clear narrative structure, and a large amount of dialogues, which enrich with oral register the literary style of this corpus. The English version of this corpus was originally built as benchmark data-set to test how well language models capture meaning in context. It contains 108 books, and a vocabulary size of 53,628.

French version of CBT, named CBT-fr, was constructed to guarantee enough linguistic similarities between the collected books in the two languages. 104 freely available books were included. One third of the books were purposely chosen because they were classical translations of English literary classics. Chapter heads, titles, notes and

[1] ORFEO corpus available at `www.cocoon.huma-num.fr/exist/crdo/` ; Rhapsodie corpus at `www.projet-rhapsodie.fr`.

[2] Corpus available at `www.cnrtl.fr/corpus/estrepublicain/`.

[3] Script available at `https://github.com/attardi/wikiextractor`.

[4] At the time being, this part of CaBeRnet corpus is still subject to Licence restrictions. This restricted amount of AFP news reports can reasonably fall in the public domain.

[5] TALN proceedings corpus (about 2 million) builds on a subset of 586 scientific articles (from 2007 to 2013), namely TALN and RECITAL. Available at `redac.univ-tlse2.fr/corpus/taln_en.html`.

[6] This data-set can be found at `www.fb.ai/babi/`.

all types of editorial information were removed to obtain a plain narrative text. The effort of keeping proportion, genre, domain, and time as equal as possible yields a multilingual set of comparable corpora with a similar balance and representativeness.

CHILDREN BOOK TEST - FR	WORDS
number of different lemmas	25 139
total number of forms	95 058
mean number of forms per lemma	3.78
Number of lemmas having more than one form :	14 128
Percentage of lemmas with multiple forms	56.20

Table 2: Lexical statistics of French CBT, performed as described in §3.

3. Corpora Descriptive Comparison

We used two different tokenizers: SEM, Segmenteur-Étiqueteur Markovien standalone Dupont (2017) and TreeTagger. Both are based on cascades of regular expressions, and both perform tokenization and sentence splitting. The first was used for descriptive purposes because it technically allowed to segment and tokenize all corpora including OSCAR (23 billion words). Hence, all corpora were entirely segmented into sentences and tokenized using SEM. The second tokenization method was run only on 3 million words samples to automatically tag them with TreeTagger into part-of-speech and lemmatize them.[7] All corpora were randomly shuffled by sentence to then select samples of 3 million words, to be able to compare them in terms of lexical composition (Type-Token Ratio, see Table 4).

3.1. Corpora Size and Composition

Length of sentences is a simple measure to quantify both sentence syntactic complexity and genre. Hence, the number of sentences reported in Table 3 shows interesting patterns of distributions across genres, consider the comparison between CaBeRnet an Wiki-fr. In our effort to evaluate the impact of corpora pre-training on ELMo-based contextualized word-embedding, we introduce here our two terms of comparison, namely the crawled corpus OSCAR-fr and the Wikipedia-fr one.

3.1.1. OSCAR fr

As it has been shown that pre-trained language models can be significantly improved by using more data (Liu et al., 2019; Raffel et al., 2019), we decided to include in our comparison a corpus of French text extracted from Common Crawl[8]. We leverage on a recently published corpus, OSCAR (Ortiz Suárez et al., 2019), which offers a pre-classified and pre-filtered version of the November 2018 Common Craw snapshot.

[7]Based on the tag-set available at https://www.cis.uni-muenchen.de/~schmid/tools/TreeTagger/data/french-tagset.html.

[8]More information available at https://commoncrawl.org/about/.

OSCAR gathers a set of monolingual text extracted from Common Crawl - in plain text *WET* format - where all HTML tags are removed and all text encodings are converted to UTF-8. It follows a similar approach to (Grave et al., 2018) by using a language classification model based on the fastText linear classifier (Joulin et al., 2016; Grave et al., 2017) pre-trained on Wikipedia, Tatoeba and SETimes, supporting 176 different languages.

After language classification, a deduplication step is performed without introducing a specialized filtering scheme: paragraphs containing 100 or more UTF-8 encoded characters are kept. This makes OSCAR an example of unfiltered data that is nearly as noisy as to the original Crawled data.

3.1.2. FrWIKI

This corpus collects a selection of pages from Wikipedia-fr from a dump executed in April 2019, where HTML tags and tables were removed, together with template expansion using Attardi's tool (WikiExtractor, §2.1.). As reported on Table 3, in this data-set (660 million words) sentences are relatively longer compared to other corpora. It has the advantage of having a comparable size to CaBeRnet, but its homogeneity in terms of written genre is set to Wikipedia entries descriptive style.

CORPUS	WORDFORMS	TOKENS	SENTENCES
OSCAR-fr	23 212 459 287	27 439 082 933	1 003 261 066
Wiki-fr	665 599 545	802 283 130	21 775 351
CaBeRnet	697 119 013	830 894 133	54 216 010
CBT-fr	5 697 584	6 910 201	317 239

Table 3: Comparing the corpora under study.

3.2. Corpora Lexical Variety

Focusing on a useful measure of complexity that documents lexical richness or variety in vocabulary, we present the type-token ration (TTR) of the corpora under analysis. Generally used to asses language use aspects like the variety of different words used to communicate by learners or children, it represents the total number of unique words (types/forms) divided by the total number of tokens in a given sample of language production. Hence, the closer the TTR ratio is to 1, the greater the lexical richness of the corpus. Table 1 summarizes the lexical variety of the five subportions of CaBeRnet, respectively taken as representative of Oral, Popular, Fiction, News, and Academic genres. Domain diversity of texts can be observed in the lexical statistics showing a gradual increase in the number of distinct lexical forms (cf. TTR). This pattern reflects a generally acknowledged distributional pattern of vocabulary-size across genres. Oral style shows a poorer lexical variety compared to newspapers/magazines' textual typology. The lexically rich fictional/classic literature is outreached by academic writing-style with its wide-ranging specialized vocabulary. All in all, Table 1 quantitatively demonstrates that the selected textual and oral materials are indeed representative of the five types of genres of CaBeRnet.

3.3. Corpora Morphological richness

To select a measure that would help quantifying the different corpora morphological richness, we follow (Bonami and Beniamine, 2015). Hence, the proportion of lemmas with multiple forms in a given vocabulary size was evaluated on randomly selected samples of 3-million-words from each corpus under analysis (see Table 4).

3 M SAMPLES	CBT-FR	CABERNET	FR-WIKI	OSCAR
nb of diff. lemmas	25 139	30 488	31 385	31 204
tot. nb forms	95 058	180 089	238 121	190 078
mean nb forms/lemma	3.78	6.19	7.85	6.40
nb lemmas > 1 form	14 128	15 927	15 182	16 480
% lemmas > 1 form	56.20	52.24	48.37	52.81

Table 4: Lexical statistics on morphological richness over randomly selected samples of 3 million words from each corpus. nb : number

Table 4 reports some more in-depth lexical and morphological statistics across corpora. Although OSCAR is 34 times bigger than CaBeRnet, their total number of forms and the proportion of lemmas having more than one form in a 3-million-word sample are comparable. FrWiki shows a radically different lexical distribution with numerous hapaxes but a lower morphological richness. Although its total number of forms is more than one third higher than in OSCAR and CaBeRnet samples, the proportion of lemmas having more than one distinct form is around four points below CaBeRnet and OSCAR. Comparatively, youth literature in CBT-fr shows the greatest morphological richness, around 56% of lemmas have more than one form.

4. Corpora Evaluation Tasks

This section reports the method of experiments designed to better understand the computational impact of the quality, size and linguistic balance of ELMo's (Peters et al., 2018) pre-training (§4.1.) and their evaluations tasks (§4.3.).

Embeddings from Language Models ELMo is an LSTM-based language model. More precisely, it uses a bidirectional language model, which combines a both forward and a backward LSTM-based language models. ELMo also computes a context-independent token representation via a CNN over characters. Methodologically, we selected ELMo which not only performs generally better on sequence tagging than other architectures, but which is also better suited to pre-train on small corpora because of its smaller number of parameters (93.6 million) compared to the RoBERTa-base architecture used for CamBERT (BERTbase, 12,110 million - Transformer) (Martin et al., 2019).

4.1. ELMo Pre-traing & Fine-tuning Method

Two protocols were carried out to evaluate the impact of corpora characteristics on the tasks under analysis. *Method 1* implies a full pre-training ELMo-based language models for each of the corpora mentioned in Table 3. While *Method 2* is based on pre-training OSCAR + fine-tuning with our French Balanced Reference Corpus CaBeRnet, yielding $\text{ELMo}_{\text{OSCAR+CaBeRnet}}$. Hence, the pure pre-traing (i.e. Method 1) yields the following four language models which were pre-trained on the four corpora under comparison : $\text{ELMo}_{\text{OSCAR}}$, $\text{ELMo}_{\text{Wikipedia}}$, $\text{ELMo}_{\text{CaBeRnet}}$ and ELMo_{CBT}.

4.2. Base evaluation systems

UDPipe Future (Straka, 2018) is an LSTM based model ranked 3rd in dependency parsing and 6th in POS tagging during the CoNLL 2018 shared task (Seker et al., 2018). We report the scores as they appear in Kondratyuk (2019)'s paper. We add to UDPipe Future, five differently trained ELMo language model pre-trained on the qualitatively and quantitatively different corpora under comparison. Additionally, we also test the impact of the CaBeRnet Corpus on ELMo fine-tuning.

The LSTM-CRF is a model originally concived by Lample et al. (2016) is just a Bi-LSTM pre-appended by both character level word embeddings and pre-trained word embeddings and pos-appended by a CRF decoder layer. For our experiments, we use the implementation of (Straková et al., 2019) which is readily available[9] and it is designed to easily pre-append contextualized word-embeddings to the model.

4.3. Evaluation Tasks

We distinguish three main evaluation tasks that were performed to asses the lexical and syntactic quality of contextualized word-embeddings obtained from different pretraining corpora under comparison.Crucially, comparing them with and ELMo pre-trained on OSCAR and fine-tuned with CaBeRnet, i.e. $\text{ELMo}_{\text{OSCAR+CaBeRnet}}$, will allow to control for the presence of oral transcriptions and proceeding in order to understand its impact on the accuracy of our language model and on the development experiments after fine-tuning.

Syntactic tasks The evaluation tasks were selected to probe to what extent corpus "representativeness" and balance is impacting syntactic representations, in both (1) low-level syntactic relations in POS-tagging tasks, and (2) higher level syntactic relations at constituent- and sentence-level thanks to dependency-parsing evaluation task. Namely, POS-tagging is a low-level syntactic task, which consists in assigning to each word its corresponding grammatical category. Dependency-parsing consists of higher order syntactic task like predicting the labeled syntactic tree capturing the syntactic relations between words. We evaluate the performance of our models using the standard UPOS accuracy for POS-tagging, and Unlabeled Attachment Score (UAS) and Labeled Attachment Score (LAS) for dependency parsing. We assume gold tokenisation and gold word segmentation as provided in the UD treebanks.

Lexical tasks To test for word-level representation obtained through the different pre-training corpora and finetunings, Named Entity Recognition task (NER) was retained (4.3.2.). As it involves a sequence labeling task that

[9]Available at `https://github.com/ufal/acl2019_nested_ner`.

Treebank	Tokens	Words	Sentences	Genre
GSD	389 363	400 387	16 342	News Wiki. Blogs
Sequoia	68 615	70 567	3 099	Pop. Wiki. Med. EuroParl
Spoken	34 972	34 972	2 786	Oral transcip.
ParTUT	27 658	28 594	1 020	Oral Wiki. Legal

Table 5: Sizes of the 4 treebanks used in the evaluations of POS-tagging and dependency parsing.

consists in predicting which words refer to real-world objects, such as people, locations, artifacts and organizations, it directly probes the quality and specificity of semantic representations issued by the more or less balanced corpora under comparison.

4.3.1. POS-tagging and dependency parsing

Experiments were run using the Universal Dependencies (UD) paradigm and its corresponding UD POS-tag set (Petrov et al., 2011) and UD treebank collection version 2.2 (Nivre et al., 2018), which was used for the CoNLL 2018 shared task.
Different terms of comparisons were considered on the two downstream tasks of part-of-speech (POS) tagging and dependency parsing.

Treebanks test data-set We perform our work on the four freely available French UD treebanks in UD v2.2: GSD, Sequoia, Spoken, and ParTUT, presented in Table 5.
GSD treebank (McDonald et al., 2013) is the second-largest tree-bank available for French after the FTB (described in subsection 4.3.2.), it contains data from blogs, news, reviews, and Wikipedia.
Sequoia tree-bank (Candito et al., 2014) comprises more than 3000 sentences, from the French Europarl, the regional newspaper *L'Est Républicain*, the French Wikipedia and documents from the European Medicines Agency.
Spoken was automatically converted from the Rhapsodie tree-bank (Lacheret et al., 2014) with manual corrections. It consists of 57 sound samples of spoken French with phonetic transcription aligned with sound (word boundaries, syllables, and phonemes), syntactic and prosodic annotations.
Finally, **ParTUT** is a conversion of a multilingual parallel treebank developed at the University of Turin, and consisting of a variety of text genres, including talks, legal texts, and Wikipedia articles, among others; ParTUT data is derived from the already-existing parallel treebank, Par(allel)TUT (Sanguinetti and Bosco, 2015). Table 5 contains a summary comparing the sizes of the treebanks.

State-of-the-art For POS-tagging and Parsing we select as a baseline UDPipe Future (2.0), without any additional contextualized embeddings (Straka, 2018). This model was ranked 3rd in dependency parsing and 6th in POS-tagging during the CoNLL 2018 shared task (Seker et al., 2018). Notably, UDPipe Future provides us a strong baseline that does not make use of any pre-trained contextual embedding.
We report on Table 6 the published results on UDify by (Kondratyuk, 2019), a multitask and multilingual model based on mBERT that is near state-of-the-art on all UD languages including French for both POS-tagging and dependency parsing.
Finally, it is also relevant to compare our results with CamemBERT on the selected tasks, because compared to UDify it is the work that pushed the furthest the performance in fine-tuning end-to-end a BERT-based model.

4.3.2. Named Entity Recognition

Treebanks test data-set The benchmark data set from the French Treebank (FTB) (Abeillé et al., 2003) was selected in its 2008 version, as introduced by Candito and Crabbé (2009) and complemented with NER annotations by Sagot et al. (2012)[10]. The tree-bank, shows a large proportion of the entity mentions that are multi-word entities. We therefore report the three metrics that are commonly used to evaluate models: precision, recall, and F1 score.

NER State-of-the-art English has received the most attention in NER in the past, with some recent developments in German, Dutch and Spanish by Straková et al. (2019). In French, no extensive work has been done due to the limited availability of NER corpora. We compare our model with the stable baselines settled by (Dupont, 2018), who trained both CRF and BiLSTM-CRF architectures on the FTB and enhanced them using heuristics and pre-trained word-embeddings.
And additional term of comparison was identified in a recently released state-of-the-art language model for French, CamemBERT (Martin et al., 2019), based on the RoBERTa architecture pre-trained on the French sub-corpus of the newly available multilingual corpus OSCAR (Ortiz Suárez et al., 2019).

5. Results & Discussion

5.1. Dependency Parsing and POS-tagging

$\text{ELMo}_{\text{CaBeRnet}}$: a test for balance The word-embeddings representations offered by $\text{ELMo}_{\text{CaBeRnet}}$ are not only competitive but sometimes better than Wikipedia ones. One should keep in mind that almost all of the four treebanks we use in this section include Wikipedia data. $\text{ELMo}_{\text{CaBeRnet}}$ is reaching state-of-the-are results in POS-tagging on Spoken. Notably, it performs better than CamemBERT, the previous state of the art on this oral specialized tree-bank (cf. dark gray highlight on Table 6). We understand this results as a clear effect of balance when testing upon a purely spoken test-set. Importantly, this effect is difficultly explainable by the size of oral-style data in CaBeRnet. The oral sub-part is only one fifth of the total, and in this one fifth, only an even smaller amount of data comes from purely oral transcripts comparable the ones in the Spoken tree-bank, namely 67,444 words from Rhapsodie corpus, and 575,894 words form ORFEO. Hence, CaBeRnet's balanced oral language use shows to pay off in POS-tagging. These results are extremely surprising especially given the fact that

[10]The NER-annotated FTB contains approximately than 12k sentences, and more than 350k tokens were extracted from articles of *Le Monde* newspaper (1989 - 1995). As a whole, it encompasses 11,636 entity mentions distributed among 7 different types : 2025 mentions of "Person", 3761 of "Location", 2382 of "Organisation", 3357 of "Company", 67 of "Product", 15 of "POI" (Point of Interest) and 29 of "Fictional Character".

Model	GSD			Sequoia			Spoken			ParTUT		
	UPOS	UAS	LAS	UPOS	UAS	LAS	UPOS	UAS	LAS	UPOS	UAS	LAS
Baseline UDPipe Future	97.63	90.65	88.06	98.79	92.37	90.73	95.91	82.90	77.53	96.93	92.17	89.63
+ELMo$_{CBT}$	97.49	90.21	87.37	98.40	92.18	90.56	96.60	85.05	79.82	97.27	92.55	90.44
+ELMo$_{Wikipedia}$	97.92	92.13	89.77	99.22	94.28	92.97	97.28	85.61	80.79	**97.62**	94.01	91.78
+ELMo$_{CaBeRnet}$	97.87	92.02	89.62	99.33	94.42	93.14	*97.30*	85.39	80.63	97.43	94.02	91.86
+ELMo$_{OSCAR}$	97.85	92.41	90.05	99.30	94.43	93.25	97.10	85.83	**80.94**	97.47	**94.74**	**92.55**
+ELMo$_{OSCAR+CaBeRnet}$	**97.98**	**92.57**	**90.22**	**99.34**	**94.51**	**93.38**	97.24	**85.91**	80.93	97.58	94.47	92.05
State-of-the-art												
UDify	97.83	93.60	91.45	97.89	92.53	90.05	96.23	85.24	80.01	96.12	90.55	88.06
UDPipe Future + mBERT	97.98	92.55	90.31	*99.32*	94.88	93.81	97.23	*86.27*	*81.40*	*97.64*	94.51	92.47
CamemBERT	*98.19*	*94.82*	*92.47*	99.21	*95.56*	*94.39*	96.68	86.05	80.07	97.63	95.21	*92.90*

Table 6: Final POS and dependency parsing scores on 4 French treebanks (French GSD, Spoken, Sequoia and ParTUT), reported on test sets (4 averaged runs) assuming gold tokenisation. Best scores in bold, second to best underlined, state-of-the-art results in italics.

NER - Results on FTB	Precision	Recall	F1
Baselines Models			
SEM (CRF) (Dupont, 2018)	87.89	82.34	85.02
LSTM-CRF (Dupont, 2018)	87.23	83.96	85.57
LSTM-CRF test models	85.87	81.35	83.55
+FastText	88.53	84.63	86.53
+FastText+ELMo$_{CBT}$	79.77	77.63	78.69
+FastText+ELMo$_{Wikipedia}$	88.87	87.56	88.21
+FastText+ELMo$_{CaBeRnet}$	88.91	87.22	88.06
+FastText+ELMo$_{OSCAR}$	88.89	88.43	88.66
+FastText+ELMo$_{OSCAR+CaBeRnet}$	**90.70**	**89.12**	**89.93**
State-of-the-art Models			
CamemBERT (Martin et al., 2019)	88.35	87.46	87.93

Table 7: NER Results on French Treebank (FTB): **best scores**, second to best.

our evaluation method was aiming at comparing the quality of word-embedding representations and not beating the state-of-the-art.

ELMo$_{CaBeRnet}$: a test for coverage From Table 6, we discover that not only balance, but also the broad and diverse genre converge of CaBeRnet may play a role in its POS-tagging success is we compare its results with ELMo$_{CBT}$ that also features oral dialogues in youth literature. The fact that ELMo$_{CBT}$ does not show a comparable performance in POS-tagging, can be interpreted as linked to its size, but possibly also to its lack of variety in genres, thus, suggesting the advantage of a comprehensive coverage of language use. This suggests that a balanced sample may enhance the convergence of generalization about oral-style from distinct genre that still imply oral-like dialogues like in fiction. In sum, broad coverage may contribute to enhancing representations about oral language.

The effect of balance on Fine-tuning For POS-tagging in GSD the results of ELMo$_{OSCAR}$ are in second place position compared to ELMo$_{OSCAR+CaBeRnet}$ that is extremely close to ELMo$_{Wikipedia}$. While in POS-tagging in ParTUT, ELMo$_{Wikipedia}$ exhibits better results than ELMo$_{OSCAR}$, and ELMo$_{OSCAR+CaBeRnet}$ is in second position.

Further comparing GSD and Sequoia scores from ELMo$_{OSCAR}$ and ELMo$_{OSCAR+CaBeRnet}$, we observe that fine-tuning with CaBeRnet the emdeddings that were pre-trained on OSCAR, yields better representations for the three tasks compared to both the original ELMo$_{OSCAR}$ and ELMo$_{CaBeRnet}$. However, fine-tuning does not always yield better findings than ELMo$_{OSCAR}$ on Spoken and ParTUT, where ELMo$_{OSCAR+CaBeRnet}$ places in second after ELMo$_{OSCAR}$ for parsing scores UAS/LAS (cf. Table 6).

A closer look on Parsing results reveals an interesting pattern of results across treebanks (see light gray highlights on Table 6). We see that for GSD and Sequoia the CaBeRnet fine-tuned version ELMo$_{OSCAR+CaBeRnet}$ compared to the pure OSCAR pre-trained ELMo$_{OSCAR}$ is achieving higher scores. While a reverse and less clear-cut pattern is observable for the other two treebanks, namely Spoken and ParTUT. This configuration can be explained if we understand this pattern as due to the reinforcement and unlearning of ELMo$_{OSCAR}$ representations during the process of fine-tuning. Specifically, we can observe that parsing scores are better on treebanks that share the kind of language use represented in CaBeRnet, while they are worst on corpora that are closer in language sample to OSCAR corpus, like Spoken and ParTuT. This calls for further developments of CaBeRnet (§6.).

ELMo$_{CBT}$: small but relevant ELMo$_{CBT}$ shows an intriguing pattern of results. Even if its scores are under the baseline on GSD and Sequoia, it yields over the baseline results for Spoken and ParTUT. Given its reduced size, one would expect it to overfit, this would explain the under baseline performance. However, this was not the case on Spoken and ParTUT treebanks, thus showing ELMo$_{CBT}$ contribution in generating representations that are useful to UDPipe model to achieve better results in POS-tagging and parsing tasks on the ParTUT and Spoken tree-banks. The presence of oral dialogues is certainly playing a role in this results' pattern. This unexpected result calls for further investigation on the impact of pre-training with reduced-size, noiseless, domain-specific corpora.

5.2. NER

For named entity recognition, LSTM-CRF +FastText +ELMo$_{OSCAR+CaBeRnet}$ achieves a better precision, recall and F1 than the traditional CRF-based SEM architectures (§ 4.3.2.) and CamemBERT, which is currently state-of-the-art.Importantly, LSTM-CRF +FastText +ELMo$_{\text{CaBeRnet}}$ reaches better results in finding entity mentions, than Wikipedia which is a highly specialized corpus in terms of vocabulary variety and size, as can be seen in the overwhelming total number of unique forms it contains (see Table 4). We can conclude that both pre-training and fine-tuning with CaBeRnet on ELMo OSCAR generates better word-embedding representations than Wikipedia in this downstream task.

CBT-fr NER results are under the LSTM-CRF baseline. This can possibly be explained by the distance in terms of topics and domain from FTB tree-bank (i.e. newspaper articles), or by the reduced-size of the corpus to yield good-enough representation to perform entity mentions recognition.

All in all, our evaluations confirm the effectiveness of large ELMo-based language models fine-tuned or pre-trained with a balanced and linguistically representative corpus, like CaBeRnet as opposed to domain-specific ones, or to an extra-large and noisy one like OSCAR.

6. Perspectives & Conclusion

The paper investigates the relevance of different types of corpora on ELMo's pre-training and fine-tuning. It confirms the effectiveness and quality of word-embeddings obtained through balanced and linguistically representative corpora.

By adding to UDPipe Future 5 differently trained ELMo language models that were pre-trained on qualitatively and quantitatively different corpora, our French Balanced Reference Corpus CaBeRnet unexpectedly establishes a new state-of-the-art for POS-tagging over previous monolingual (Straka, 2018) and multilingual approaches (Straka et al., 2019; Kondratyuk, 2019).

The proposed evaluation methods are showing that the two newly built corpora that are published here are not only relevant for neural NLP and language modeling in French, but that corpus balance shows to be a significant predictor of ELMo's accuracy on Spoken test data-set and for NER tasks.

Other perspective uses of CaBeRnet involve it use as a corpus offering a reference point for lexical frequency measures, like association measures. Its comparability with English COCA further grants the cross-linguistic validity of measures like Point-wise Mutual Information or DICE's Coefficient. The representativeness probed through our experimental approach are key aspects that allow such measures to be tested against psycho-linguistic and neuro-linguistic data as shown in previous neuro-imaging studies (Fabre et al., 2018).

The results obtained for the parsing tasks on ParTUT open a new perspective for the development of the French Balanced Reference Corpus, involving the enhancement of the terminological coverage of CaBeRnet. A sixth sub-part could be included to cover technical domains like legal and medical ones, and thereby enlarge the specialized lexical coverage of CaBeRnet. Further developments of this resource would involve an extension to cover user-generated content, ranging from well written blogs, tweets to more variable written productions like newspaper's comment or forums, as present in the CoMeRe corpus (Chanier et al., 2014).The computational experiments conducted here also show that pre-training language models like ELMo on a very small sample like the French Children Book Test corpus or CaBeRnet yields unexpected results. This opens a perspective for languages that have smaller training corpora. ELMo could be a better suited language model for those languages than it is for others having larger size resources.

Results on the NER task show that size - usually presented as the more important factor to enhance the precision of representation of word-embeddings - matters less than linguistic representativeness, as achieved through corpus linguistic balance. ELMo$_{\text{OSCAR+CaBeRnet}}$ sets state-of-the art results in NER (i.e. Precision, Recall and F1) that are superior than those obtained with a 30 times larger corpus, like OSCAR.

To conclude, our current evaluations show that linguistic quality in terms of *representativeness* and balance is yielding better performing contextualized word-embeddings.

Acknowledgments

We acknowledge Benoit Crabbé for his helpful suggestions at the beginning of reflection on balanced corpora. We are indebted to Yoann Dupont for his help in collecting data from Wikimedia dumps and for his critical comments. Olivier Bonami and Kim Gerdes conversations were instrumental. This work was supported by the French National Research Agency (ANR) under grant ANR-14-CERA-0001 and BASNUM (ANR-18-CE38-0003). The authors are grateful to Inria Sophia Antipolis - Méditerranée "Nef" computation cluster for providing resources and support.

Bibliographical References

Abeillé, A., Clément, L., and Toussenel, F., (2003). *Building a Treebank for French*, pages 165–187. Kluwer, Dordrecht.

Baroni, M., Bernardini, S., Ferraresi, A., and Zanchetta, E. (2009). The wacky wide web: A collection of very large linguistically processed web-crawled corpora. *Language Resources and Evaluation*, 43:209–226, 09.

Douglas Biber, editor. (1993). *Representativeness in Corpus Design.* In: Literary and Linguistic Computing 8.4.

Bonami, O. and Beniamine, S. (2015). Implicative structure and joint predictiveness. In Vito Pirelli, et al., editors, *Word Structure and Word Usage. Proceedings of the NetWordS Final Conference*, Pisa, Italy.

Burnard, L. (2007). 520 million words, 1990-present. In *The British National Corpus, version 3 - BNC XML Edition.*

Candito, M. and Crabbé, B. (2009). Improving generative statistical parsing with semi-supervised word clustering. In *Proc. of IWPT'09*, Paris, France.

Candito, M., Perrier, G., Guillaume, B., Ribeyre, C., Fort, K., Seddah, D., and de la Clergerie, É. V. (2014). Deep syntax annotation of the sequoia french treebank. In Nicoletta Calzolari, et al., editors, *Proceedings of the Ninth International Conference on Language Resources and Evaluation, LREC 2014, Reykjavik, Iceland, May 26-31, 2014.*, pages 2298–2305. European Language Resources Association (ELRA).

Chanier, T., Poudat, C., Sagot, B., Antoniadis, G., Wigham, C. R., Hriba, L., Longhi, J., and Seddah, D. (2014). The CoMeRe corpus for French: structuring and annotating heterogeneous CMC genres. *JLCL - Journal for Language Technology and Computational Linguistics*, 29(2):1–30. Final version to Special Issue of JLCL (Journal of Language Technology and Computational Linguistics (JLCL, http://jlcl.org/): BUILDING AND ANNOTATING CORPORA OF COMPUTER-MEDIATED DISCOURSE: Issues and Challenges at the Interface of Corpus and Computational Linguistics (ed. by Michael Beißwenger, Nelleke Oostdijk, Angelika Storrer & Henk van den Heuvel).

Davies, M. (2008). 520 million words, 1990-present. In *The Corpus of Contemporary American English (COCA)*.

Dupont, Y. (2017). Exploration de traits pour la reconnaissance d'entités nommées du français par apprentissage automatique. In *24e Conférence sur le Traitement Automatique des Langues Naturelles (TALN)*, page 42.

Dupont, Y. (2018). Exploration de traits pour la reconnaissance d'entit'es nomm'ees du français par apprentissage automatique. In *24e Conf'erence sur le Traitement Automatique des Langues Naturelles (TALN)*, page 42.

Fabre, M., Bhattasali, S., and Hale, J. (2018). Processing mwes: Neurocognitive bases of verbal mwes and lexical cohesiveness within mwes. In *Proceedings of the 14th Workshop on Multiword Expressions (COLING 2018), Santa Fe, NM.*

Grave, E., Mikolov, T., Joulin, A., and Bojanowski, P. (2017). Bag of tricks for efficient text classification. In Mirella Lapata, et al., editors, *Proceedings of the 15th Conference of the European Chapter of the Association for Computational Linguistics, EACL 2017, Valencia, Spain, April 3-7, 2017, Volume 2: Short Papers*, pages 427–431. Association for Computational Linguistics.

Grave, E., Bojanowski, P., Gupta, P., Joulin, A., and Mikolov, T. (2018). Learning word vectors for 157 languages. In Nicoletta Calzolari, et al., editors, *Proceedings of the Eleventh International Conference on Language Resources and Evaluation, LREC 2018, Miyazaki, Japan, May 7-12, 2018.* European Language Resources Association (ELRA).

Hill, F., Bordes, A., Chopra, S., and Weston, J. (2015). The goldilocks principle: Reading children's books with explicit memory representations.

Joulin, A., Grave, E., Bojanowski, P., Douze, M., Jégou, H., and Mikolov, T. (2016). Fasttext.zip: Compressing text classification models. *CoRR*, abs/1612.03651.

Koehn, P. (2005). Europarl: A Parallel Corpus for Statistical Machine Translation. In *Conference Proceedings: the tenth Machine Translation Summit*, pages 79–86, Phuket, Thailand. AAMT, AAMT.

Kondratyuk, D. (2019). 75 languages, 1 model: Parsing universal dependencies universally. *CoRR*, abs/1904.02099.

Lacheret, A., Kahane, S., Beliao, J., Dister, A., Gerdes, K., Goldman, J.-P., Obin, N., Pietrandrea, P., and Tchobanov, A. (2014). Rhapsodie: a prosodic-syntactic treebank for spoken French. In *Proceedings of the Ninth International Conference on Language Resources and Evaluation (LREC'14)*, pages 295–301, Reykjavik, Iceland, May. European Language Resources Association (ELRA).

Lample, G., Ballesteros, M., Subramanian, S., Kawakami, K., and Dyer, C. (2016). Neural architectures for named entity recognition. In Kevin Knight, et al., editors, *NAACL HLT 2016, The 2016 Conference of the North American Chapter of the Association for Computational Linguistics: Human Language Technologies, San Diego California, USA, June 12-17, 2016*, pages 260–270. The Association for Computational Linguistics.

Liu, Y., Ott, M., Goyal, N., Du, J., Joshi, M., Chen, D., Levy, O., Lewis, M., Zettlemoyer, L., and Stoyanov, V. (2019). Roberta: A robustly optimized BERT pretraining approach. *CoRR*, abs/1907.11692.

Martin, L., Muller, B., Ortiz Suárez, P. J., Dupont, Y., Romary, L., Villemonte de la Clergerie, É., Seddah, D., and Sagot, B. (2019). CamemBERT: a Tasty French Language Model. *arXiv e-prints*, page arXiv:1911.03894, Nov.

McDonald, R., Nivre, J., Quirmbach-Brundage, Y., Goldberg, Y., Das, D., Ganchev, K., Hall, K., Petrov, S., Zhang, H., Täckström, O., Bedini, C., Bertomeu Castelló, N., and Lee, J. (2013). Universal dependency annotation for multilingual parsing. In *Proceedings of the 51st Annual Meeting of the Association for Computational Linguistics (Volume 2: Short Papers)*, pages 92–97, Sofia, Bulgaria, August. Association for Computational Linguistics.

Nivre, J., Abrams, M., Agić, Ž., Ahrenberg, L., Antonsen, L., Aranzabe, M. J., Arutie, G., Asahara, M., Ateyah, L., Attia, M., Atutxa, A., Augustinus, L., Badmaeva, E., Ballesteros, M., Banerjee, E., Bank, S., Barbu Mititelu, V., Bauer, J., Bellato, S., Bengoetxea, K., Bhat, R. A., Biagetti, E., Bick, E., Blokland, R., Bobicev, V., Börstell, C., Bosco, C., Bouma, G., Bowman, S., Boyd, A., Burchardt, A., Candito, M., Caron, B., Caron, G., Cebiroğlu Eryiğit, G., Celano, G. G. A., Cetin, S., Chalub, F., Choi, J., Cho, Y., Chun, J., Cinková, S., Collomb, A., Çöltekin, Ç., Connor, M., Courtin, M., Davidson, E., de Marneffe, M.-C., de Paiva, V., Diaz de Ilarraza, A., Dickerson, C., Dirix, P., Dobrovoljc, K., Dozat, T., Droganova, K., Dwivedi, P., Eli, M., Elkahky, A., Ephrem, B., Erjavec, T., Etienne, A., Farkas, R., Fernandez Alcalde, H., Foster, J., Freitas, C., Gajdošová, K., Galbraith, D., Garcia, M., Gärdenfors, M., Gerdes, K., Ginter, F., Goenaga, I., Gojenola, K., Gökırmak, M., Goldberg, Y., Gómez Guinovart, X., Gonzáles Saavedra, B., Grioni, M., Grūzītis, N., Guillaume, B., Guillot-Barbance, C., Habash, N., Hajič, J., Hajič jr., J., Hà Mỹ, L., Han, N.-R., Harris, K., Haug, D., Hladká, B., Hlaváčová, J., Hociung, F., Hohle, P., Hwang, J., Ion, R., Irimia, E., Jelínek, T., Johannsen, A., Jørgensen, F., Kaşıkara, H., Kahane, S., Kanayama, H., Kanerva, J., Kayadelen, T., Kettnerová, V., Kirchner, J., Kotsyba, N., Krek, S., Kwak, S., Laippala, V., Lambertino, L., Lando, T., Larasati, S. D., Lavrentiev, A., Lee, J., Lê Hồng, P., Lenci, A., Lertpradit, S., Leung, H., Li, C. Y., Li, J., Li, K., Lim, K., Ljubešić, N., Loginova, O., Lyashevskaya, O., Lynn, T., Macketanz, V., Makazhanov, A., Mandl, M., Manning, C., Manurung, R., Mărănduc, C., Mareček, D., Marheinecke, K., Martínez Alonso, H., Martins, A., Mašek, J., Matsumoto, Y., McDonald, R., Mendonça, G., Miekka, N., Missilä, A., Mititelu, C., Miyao, Y., Montemagni, S., More, A., Moreno Romero, L., Mori, S., Mortensen, B., Moskalevskyi, B., Muischnek, K., Murawaki, Y., Müürisep, K., Nainwani, P., Navarro Horñiacek, J. I., Nedoluzhko, A., Nešpore-Bērzkalne, G., Nguyễn Thị, L., Nguyễn Thị Minh, H., Nikolaev, V., Nitisaroj, R., Nurmi, H., Ojala, S., Olúòkun, A., Omura, M., Osenova, P., Östling, R., Øvrelid, L., Partanen, N., Pascual, E., Passarotti, M., Patejuk, A., Peng, S., Perez, C.-A., Perrier, G., Petrov, S., Piitulainen, J., Pitler, E., Plank, B., Poibeau, T., Popel, M., Pretkalniņa, L., Prévost, S., Prokopidis, P., Przepiórkowski, A., Puolakainen, T., Pyysalo, S., Rääbis, A., Rademaker, A., Ramasamy, L., Rama, T., Ramisch, C., Ravishankar, V., Real, L., Reddy, S., Rehm, G., Rießler, M., Rinaldi, L., Rituma, L., Rocha, L., Romanenko, M., Rosa, R., Rovati, D., Roșca, V., Rudina, O., Sadde, S., Saleh, S., Samardžić, T., Samson, S., Sanguinetti, M., Saulīte, B., Sawanakunanon, Y., Schneider, N., Schuster, S., Seddah, D., Seeker, W., Seraji, M., Shen, M., Shimada, A., Shohibussirri, M., Sichinava, D., Silveira, N., Simi, M., Simionescu, R., Simkó, K., Šimková, M., Simov, K., Smith, A., Soares-Bastos, I., Stella, A., Straka, M., Strnadová, J., Suhr, A., Sulubacak, U., Szántó, Z., Taji, D., Takahashi, Y., Tanaka, T., Tellier, I., Trosterud, T., Trukhina, A., Tsarfaty, R., Tyers, F., Uematsu, S., Urešová, Z., Uria, L., Uszkoreit, H., Vajjala, S., van Niekerk, D., van Noord, G., Varga, V., Vincze, V., Wallin, L., Washington, J. N., Williams, S., Wirén, M., Woldemariam, T., Wong, T.-s., Yan, C., Yavrumyan, M. M., Yu, Z., Žabokrtský, Z., Zeldes, A., Zeman, D., Zhang, M., and Zhu, H. (2018). Universal dependencies 2.2. LINDAT/CLARIN digital library at the Institute of Formal and Applied Linguistics (ÚFAL), Faculty of Mathematics and Physics, Charles University.

Ortiz Suárez, P. J., Sagot, B., and Romary, L. (2019). Asynchronous Pipeline for Processing Huge Corpora on Medium to Low Resource Infrastructures. In Piotr Bański, et al., editors, *7th Workshop on the Challenges in the Management of Large Corpora (CMLC-7)*, Cardiff, United Kingdom, July. Leibniz-Institut für Deutsche Sprache.

Peters, M. E., Neumann, M., Iyyer, M., Gardner, M., Clark, C., Lee, K., and Zettlemoyer, L. (2018). Deep contextualized word representations. In Marilyn A. Walker, et al., editors, *Proceedings of the 2018 Conference of the North American Chapter of the Association for Computational Linguistics: Human Language Technologies, NAACL-HLT 2018, New Orleans, Louisiana, USA, June 1-6, 2018, Volume 1 (Long Papers)*, pages 2227–2237. Association for Computational Linguistics.

Petrov, S., Das, D., and McDonald, R. (2011). A universal part-of-speech tagset. *arXiv preprint arXiv:1104.2086*.

Raffel, C., Shazeer, N., Roberts, A., Lee, K., Narang, S., Matena, M., Zhou, Y., Li, W., and Liu, P. J. (2019). Exploring the limits of transfer learning with a unified text-to-text transformer. *CoRR*, abs/1910.10683.

Sagot, B., Richard, M., and Stern, R. (2012). Annotation référentielle du corpus arboré de Paris 7 en entités nommées (referential named entity annotation of the paris 7 french treebank) [in french]. In Georges Antoniadis, et al., editors, *Proceedings of the Joint Conference JEP-TALN-RECITAL 2012, volume 2: TALN, Grenoble, France, June 4-8, 2012*, pages 535–542. ATALA/AFCP.

Sanguinetti, M. and Bosco, C. (2015). PartTUT: The Turin University Parallel Treebank. In Roberto Basili, et al., editors, *Harmonization and Development of Resources and Tools for Italian Natural Language Processing within the PARLI Project*, volume 589 of *Studies in Computational Intelligence*, pages 51–69. Springer.

Seker, A., More, A., and Tsarfaty, R. (2018). Universal morpho-syntactic parsing and the contribution of lexica: Analyzing the onlp lab submission to the conll 2018 shared task. In *Proceedings of the CoNLL 2018 Shared Task: Multilingual Parsing from Raw Text to Universal Dependencies*, pages 208–215.

Straka, M., Straková, J., and Hajic, J. (2019). Evaluating contextualized embeddings on 54 languages in POS tagging, lemmatization and dependency parsing. *CoRR*, abs/1908.07448.

Straka, M. (2018). UDPipe 2.0 prototype at CoNLL 2018 UD shared task. In *Proceedings of the CoNLL 2018 Shared Task: Multilingual Parsing from Raw Text to Universal Dependencies*, pages 197–207, Brussels, Belgium, October. Association for Computational Linguistics.

Straková, J., Straka, M., and Hajic, J. (2019). Neural architectures for nested NER through linearization. In Anna Korhonen, et al., editors, *Proceedings of the 57th Conference of the Association for Computational Linguistics, ACL 2019, Florence, Italy, July 28- August 2, 2019, Volume 1: Long Papers*, pages 5326–5331. Association for Computational Linguistics.

Wenzek, G., Lachaux, M.-A., Conneau, A., Chaudhary, V., Guzmán, F., Joulin, A., and Grave, E. (2019). CCNet: Extracting High Quality Monolingual Datasets from Web Crawl Data. *arXiv e-prints*, page arXiv:1911.00359, Nov.

Proceedings of he 8th Workshop on Challenges in the Management of Large Corpora, pages 24–30
Language Resources and Evaluation Conference (LREC 2020), Marseille, 11–16 May 2020

Geoparsing the Historical Gazetteers of Scotland: Accurately Computing Location in Mass Digitised Texts

Rosa Filgueira[1], Claire Grover[2], Melissa Terras[3] and Beatrice Alex[2,3]
[1] Edinburgh Parallel Compute Centre
[2] School of Informatics
[3] Edinburgh Futures Institute
University of Edinburgh
r.filgueira@epcc.ed.ac.uk, grover@inf.ed.ac.uk, M.Terras@ed.ac.uk, balex@ed.ac.uk

Abstract

This paper describes work in progress on devising automatic and parallel methods for geoparsing large digital historical textual data by combining the strengths of three natural language processing (NLP) tools, the Edinburgh Geoparser, spaCy and defoe, and employing different tokenisation and named entity recognition (NER) techniques. We apply these tools to a large collection of nineteenth century Scottish geographical dictionaries, and describe preliminary results obtained when processing this data.

Keywords: text mining, geoparsing, historical text, Gazetteers of Scotland, distributed queries, Apache Spark, digital tools

1. Introduction

Ongoing efforts towards the mass digitisation of historical collections mean that digitised historical texts are increasingly being made available at scale for research. This paper describes work in progress on devising automatic and parallel methods for geoparsing large digital historical textual data. Geoparsing means automatically tagging place names in text and resolving them to their correct latitude and longitude coordinates or gazetteer entry. We combine the strengths of three natural language processing (NLP) tools, the Edinburgh Geoparser (Grover et al., 2010)[1], spaCy[2], and defoe (Filgueira et al., 2019)[3], and employing different tokenisation and named entity recognition (NER) techniques. We apply these tools to the Gazetteers of Scotland, a large collection of nineteenth century Scottish geographical dictionaries, and describe preliminary results obtained when processing this data. Our end goals are to develop more accurate geoparsing for such historical text collections but also to make such data accessible to users, in particular scholars who may not have the necessary technical skills to build tools to analyse the text themselves.

2. Background and Related Work

Text mining large historical text collections, and making that text available for others to analyse, has been an activity much pursued at the juncture of Digital Humanities and library and archive digitisation. For example, Clifford et al. (2016) focused on analysing text with respect to commodity trading in the British Empire during the 19th century. Currently, there is a similar effort to develop and apply NLP tools to historical newspapers as part of a variety of projects including Living with Machines[4], The Viral Texts Project[5] and Oceanic Exchanges: Tracing Global Information Networks in Historical Newspaper Repositories, 1840-1914.[6]

In terms of geoparsing historical text, this area of research is relatively specialised, which means that there is limited related work. The Edinburgh Geoparser, one of the tools used for this work, has been previously adapted to work with historical and literary English text (Alex et al., 2015; Alex et al., 2019) and has been further modified or applied to a number of different text datasets (Grover and Tobin, 2014; Rupp et al., 2013; Rayson et al., 2017; Porter et al., 2018) Similar tools have applied geoparsing to historical text in other languages, e.g. historical French literary text (Moncla et al., 2017) and Swedish literary text (Borin et al., 2014).

In the context of Scotland, there is not one comprehensive historical gazetteer available for research as a downloadable resource. There is an online resource called the Gazetteer for Scotland[7] which allows users to search for and find out about places in Scotland but this data is limited to online search access only.

Our challenge here is then threefold: how can we compute spatial characteristics within historical texts? How can we be assured of the accuracy of our approaches? And how can we build our historical gazetteer of Scotland, to provide information and data for others to reuse in research and teaching?

3. The Gazetteers of Scotland

For evaluating our work, we are applying our tools to The Gazetteers of Scotland (see Table 1), a collection of twenty volumes of the most popular descriptive historical gazetteers of Scotland in the nineteenth century.[8] They are considered to be geographical dictionaries and include an alphabetic list of principal places in Scotland, including towns, counties, castles, glens, antiquities and parishes. This dataset was recently made available by the National Library of Scotland on its Data Foundry[9] which makes a

[1] https://www.ltg.ed.ac.uk/software/geoparser/
[2] https://spacy.io/
[3] https://github.com/alan-turing-institute/defoe
[4] https://livingwithmachines.ac.uk/
[5] https://viraltexts.org
[6] https://oceanicexchanges.org
[7] https://www.scottish-places.info/
[8] https://data.nls.uk/data/digitised-collections/gazetteers-of-scotland/
[9] https://data.nls.uk

series of its digitised collections publicly available.

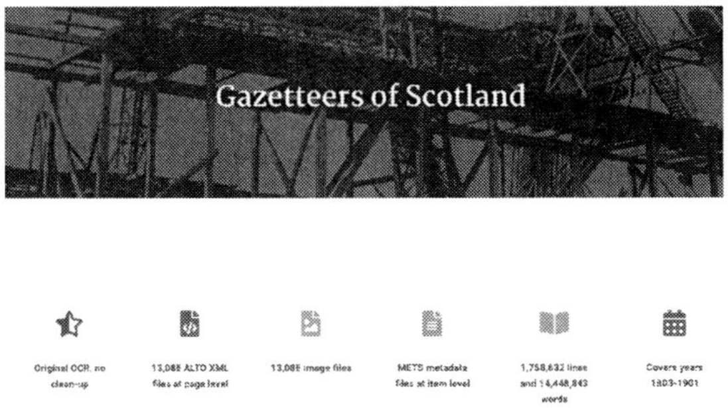

Figure 1: The Gazetteers of Scotland data on the NLS Data Foundry.

The Gazetteers of Scotland are comprised of over 13,000 page images, their OCRed text in ALTO-XML format and corresponding METS-XML format for describing the metadata for each item in the collection (see Figure 1). In total, the OCRed text amounts to almost 14.5 million words and collectively these gazetteers provide a comprehensive geographical encyclopaedia of Scotland in the nineteenth century. While this is a valuable resource, it is too time-consuming to geoparse this data manually due to its size.

Year	Title	Volumes
1803	*Gazetteer of Scotland*	1
1806	*Gazetteer of Scotland: containing a particular and concise description of the counties, parishes, islands, cities with maps*	1
1825	*Gazetteer of Scotland: arranged under the various descriptions of counties, parishes, islands*	1
1828	*Descriptive account of the principal towns in Scotland to accompany Wood's town atlas*	1
1838	*Gazetteer of Scotland with plates and maps*	2
1842	*Topographical, statistical, and historical gazetteer of Scotland*	2
1846	*Topographical dictionary of Scotland*	2
1848	*Topographical, statistical, and historical gazetteer of Scotland*	1
1868	*Imperial gazetteer of Scotland; or Dictionary of Scottish topography, compiled from the most recent authorities, and forming a complete body of Scottish geography, physical, statistical, and historical*	2
1882	*Gazetteer of Scotland*	1
1883	*Ordnance gazetteer of Scotland*	6
1901	*Ordnance gazetteer of Scotland*	1

Table 1: Gazetteers of Scotland, 1803-1901. The first column shows the publication year, the second the title and the third the number of volumes per gazetteer.

4. NLP Tools

4.1. The Edinburgh Geoparser

The Edinburgh Geoparser is a language processing tool designed to detect place name references in English text and ground them against an authoritative gazetteer so that they can be plotted on a map. The geoparser is implemented as a pipeline with two main steps (see Figure 2). The first step is geotagging, in which place name entities are identified. The second step is georesolution, which grounds place name entities against locations contained in a gazetteer. Typically, there are multiple candidates for a given place name entity, and the georesolver ranks candidates in order using various contextual clues. The georesolver allows the user to control which gazetteer to use, the main ones being GeoNames[10] or open Ordnance Survey resources, both of which we access using a service hosted by University of Edinburgh Information Services. The best choice of gazetteer will depend on the document that is being processed: if its content is global then Geonames is usually the most appropriate gazetteer but if the content is limited to Great Britain, Ordnance Survey gazetteers may help to limit the potential for ambiguity. One of the main heuristics in the georesolution step is to prefer the candidate with the largest population, but only GeoNames reliably provides this information; for this reason we have used GeoNames in this project. However, there is a way to reflect the fact that the content of the Gazetteers of Scotland is by its nature concerned primarily with Scotland by biasing disambiguation in favour of the correct Scottish places (e.g. prefer Perth, Scotland to Perth, Australia). We do this by supplying the bounding box which covers Scotland to the georesolver, which then tends to prefer candidates within the bounding box even if they have smaller populations. However, for the experiments shown in Section 5 we have not yet supplied the bounding box, but in the future we plan to do it so, so will be able compare results with and without bounding box. It is by monitoring these type of pipeline choices that we will be able to ascertain both accuracy and efficiency of our algorithmic georeferencing approaches.

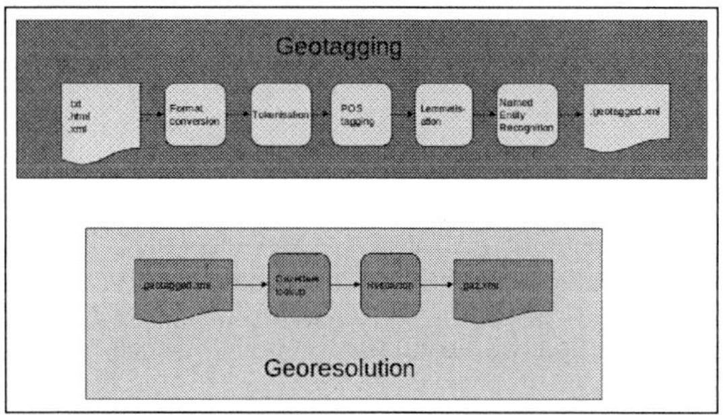

Figure 2: The Edinburgh Geoparser pipeline.

4.2. spaCy

spaCy is an open-source library for advanced Natural Language Processing in Python. It is designed specifically for production use and helps build applications that process

[10] https://www.geonames.org/

large volumes of text. Some of the features provided by spaCy are- Tokenization, Parts-of-Speech (PoS) Tagging, Text Classification and Named Entity Recognition (NER). While some of spaCy's features work independently, others require statistical models to be loaded, which enable spaCy to predict linguistic annotations. spaCy comes with two types pretrained statistical models and word vectors:

- Core models: General-purpose pretrained models to predict named entities, part-of-speech tags and syntactic dependencies.
- Starter models: Transfer learning starter packs with pretrained weights to be used as base model when training users' model. These models do not include components for specific tasks like NER or text classification.

Since the Edinburgh Geoparser gives us the flexibility to switch components, we are currently exploring the feasibility of using spaCy as one of the techniques for tokenisation and named entity recognition (NER). We have started focusing on the core models available for English [11]:

- `en_core_web_sm`: English multi-task CNN trained on OntoNotes. Assigns context-specific token vectors, POS tags, dependency parse and named entities. Small size model (11MB).
- `en_core_web_md`: English multi-task CNN trained on OntoNotes, with GloVe vectors trained on Common Crawl. Assigns word vectors, context-specific token vectors, POS tags, dependency parse and named entities. Medium size model (91MB).
- `en_core_web_lg`: English multi-task CNN trained on OntoNotes, with GloVe vectors trained on Common Crawl. Assigns word vectors, context-specific token vectors, POS tags, dependency parse and named entities. Large size model (789 MB).

To decide which spaCy model to use in our experiments, we performed an initial evaluation of the smaller and larger core models using the *Descriptive account of the principal towns in Scotland, 1828* gazetteer [12]. In this evaluation, we focused on quantifying the number of location entities identified by each model and visualising the differences between them. The `en_core_web_sm` identified 1124 locations, while `en_core_web_lg` identified 1455. Therefore, we have selected `en_core_web_lg`, since it gives us a more accurate overall results.

4.3. defoe

defoe is a scalable and portable digital toolbox for storing, processing, querying and analysing digital historical English textual data. It allows for extracting knowledge from historical text by running analyses in parallel via the Apache Spark big data framework and storing the preprocessed data (for further queries) in several storage solutions, such as an HDFS file system, an ElasticSearch distributed engine or a PostgreSQL database (see Figure 3). defoe is able to extract, transform and load (ETL) collections that comprise several XML schemas and physical representations. It offers a rich set of text mining queries to search across large-scale datasets and returns results for further analysis and interpretation. It also includes preprocessing techniques to mitigate against optical character recognition (OCR) errors and other issues (such as long-S and line-break hyphenation) and to standardise the text.

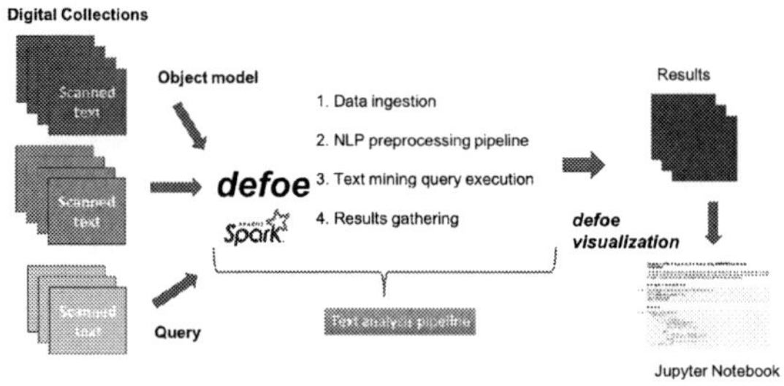

Figure 3: The defoe architecture.

defoe enables us to configure any query/queries to be submitted for an entire corpus or dataset processed, including the tokeniser and entity recogniser to use, which currently are those originally distributed within the Edinburgh Geoparser, and spaCy `en_core_web_lg` core model.

4.4. Combination of Methods

Since defoe already supports the XML schemas of the Gazetteers of Scotland, we have used it to create a new query that geoparses this collection automatically and in parallel using different geotagger options (Original geotagger from the Edinburgh Geoparser vs spaCy Name Entity) and combining them with the georesolution step of the Edinburgh Geoparser. The combined system performs the following tasks:

- Ingests the pages of all books belonging to the Gazetteers of Scotland data,
- Cleans the text to fix OCR errors caused by long-s characters and broken word tokens as a result of end-of-line hyphenation. Both steps are conducted using methods proposed and tested in (Alex et al., 2012),
- Identifies entities by employing the tokenisation and NER technique specified in the configuration file of the query,
- Applies georesolution to place name entities, and
- Groups the results by year and technique and provides them in combination with metadata associated with each book.

The first two steps of this query can be omitted if we apply the desired geoparser process to data that has been previously read, cleaned and stored using ElasticSearch. The parallelisation of the processing allows much faster turnarounds for obtaining and testing results. This is particularly useful during the method development process.

[11] `https://spacy.io/models/en`

[12] `https://github.com/alan-turing-institute/defoe_visualization/blob/master/Scottish_Gazetteer/Comparing_spacy_lang_models.ipynb`

5. Preliminary Results

We compare different settings in defoe for the named entity recognition step, either the one from the Edinburgh Geoparser or spaCy and in both cases use the Edinburgh Geoparser's resolution step to disambiguate the place names. The georesolved output for running defoe's geoparser query using the original geotagger technique[13] or spaCy[14] is available for download. To visualise these results, we have created a collection of Jupyter Notebooks[15] where we load them into Pandas Dataframes and compare the locations that we obtain with each technique. Figures 4 and 5 show the most frequent georesolved place names across the entire gazetteers collection.

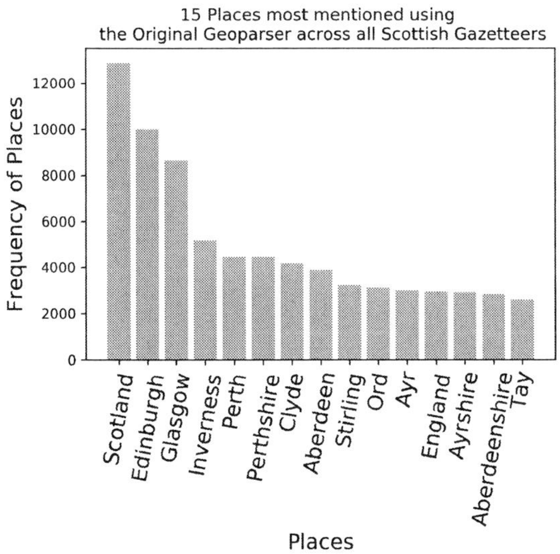

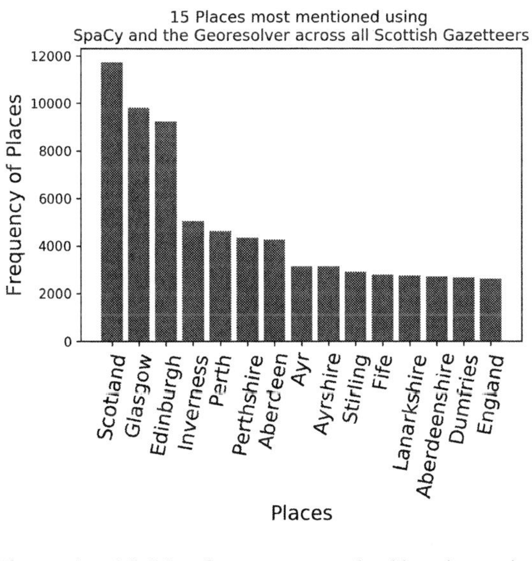

Figures 4 and 5: Most frequent georesolved locations using the Edinburgh Geoparser (above) or spaCy (below) NER.

Notice that the five most frequent locations mentioned among both techniques are *Edinburgh, Scotland, Glasgow, Inverness* and *Perth*.

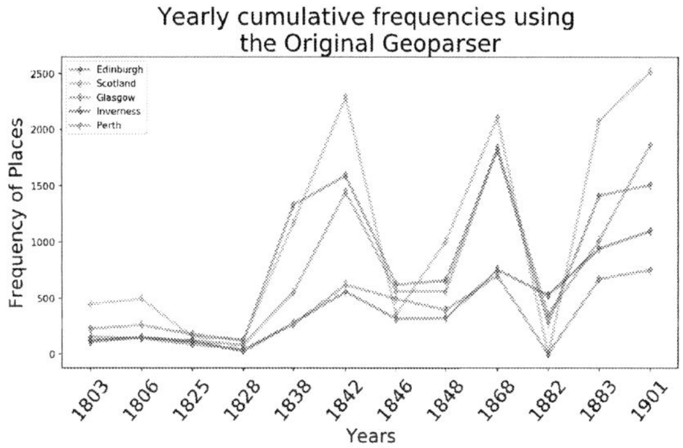

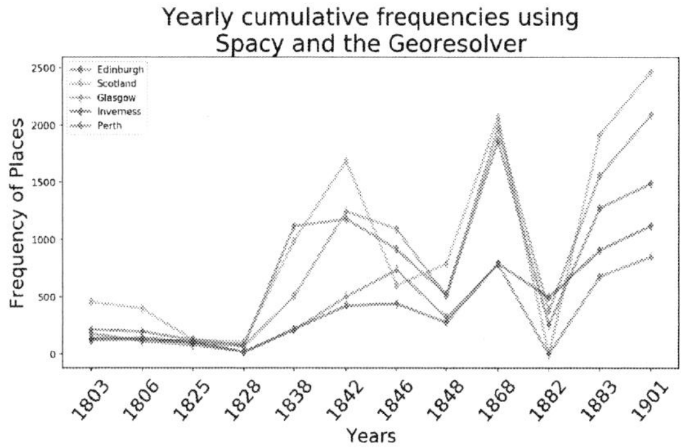

Figures 6 and 7: Cumulative frequency of the five most mentioned locations using the Edinburgh Geoparser (above) or spaCy (below) NER over the years across the full Scottish Gazetteers collection.

Figures 6 and 7 show the yearly cumulative frequencies of these five places to analyse the evolution of how often they are mentioned with each technique. For reference, Figure 8 shows the normalized frequency of words for each year, obtained using a different defoe query.

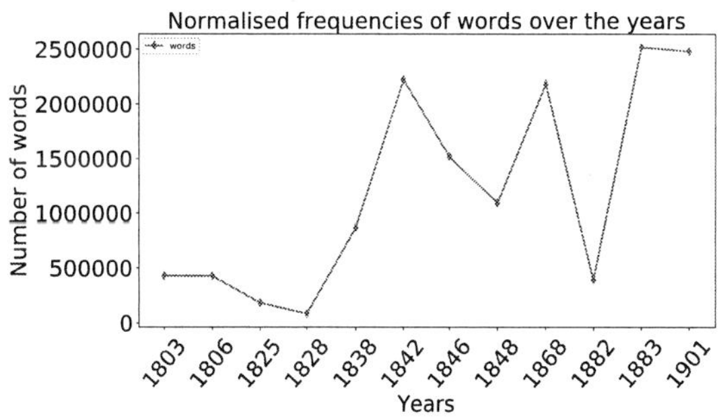

Figure 8: Normalized frequencies of words across the full Scottish Gazetteers collection.

Figures 9 and 10 show a more detailed study of the variation of locations' frequencies over the years. Both display the frequencies of the 15 most mentioned and georesolved places per year and technique.

[13] `https://drive.google.com/open?id=1T26YHz5pFAEeJal0KHe77TGoKhkxYv_S`

[14] `https://drive.google.com/open?id=1f7iD-ng6jVurG9BtqrV_ZYYJGq9o93co`

[15] `https://github.com/alan-turing-institute/defoe_visualization/blob/master/Scottish_Gazetteer`

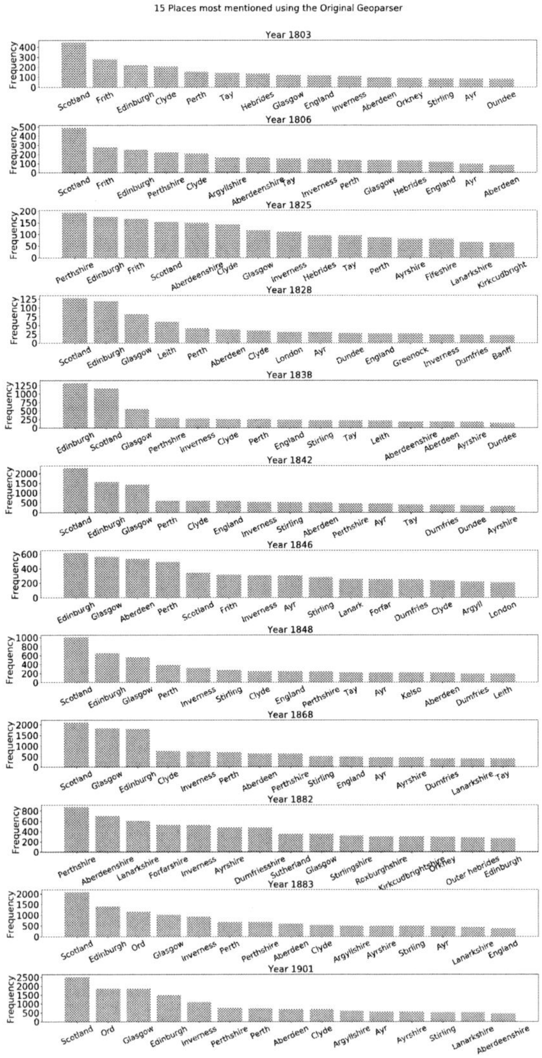

Figure 9: Most frequent georesolved locations using the Edinburgh Geoparser NER gathering the results by publication years.

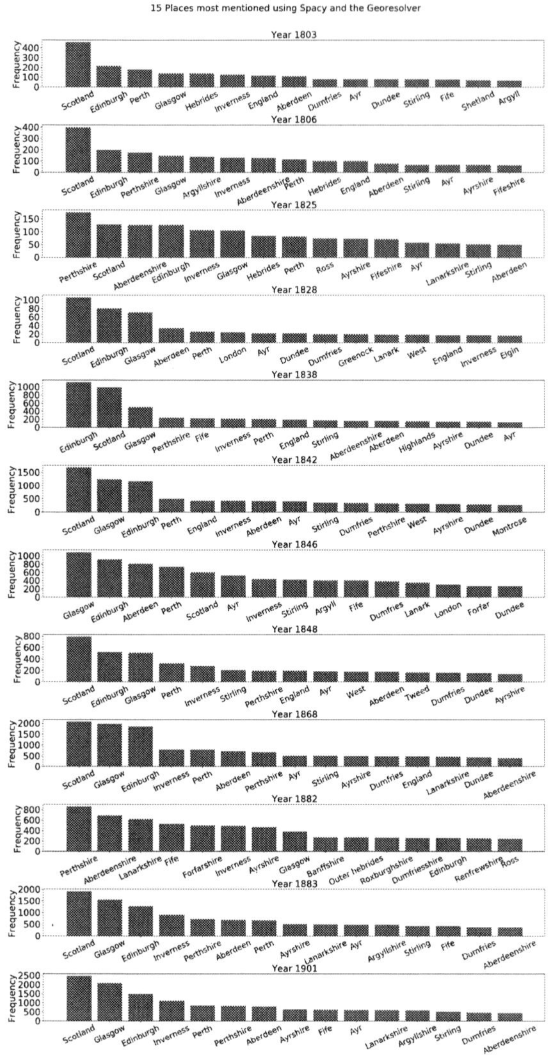

Figure 10: Most frequent georesolved locations using the spaCy NER gathering the results by publication years.

All these graphs show that the Edinburgh Geoparser is able to recognise several locations more frequently for equivalent place names.

Finally, we also explore which are the most frequent places names that have been identified but not resolved using the Edinburgh Geoparser (see Figure 11), the top four place names being Scottish shires.

We have yet to conduct a formal evaluation of the geotagging and georesolution steps on this data to see how both methods compare quantitatively and to find out where further work is needed to improve performance overall. Over the summer 2020 we plan to annotate a random subset of excerpts from the gazetteers to create a gold standard and compare it against system output. Such formal evaluation is essential to provide transparency about the accuracy of geoparsing and text mining methods developed to analyse mass digitised content automatically. We will fully document our code, and make our training set available for others, to encourage open science approaches to data analysis.

We expect that geoparsing performance on this type of data is likely to be affected by the quality of the OCR, the use of historical place name variants or spelling variation and the use of Gaelic place names. The collection contains volumes published over the course of the 19th century during which type and quality of printing and use of language changed. This is undoubtedly going to be affected by OCR quality and consistency of spellings across the volumes. Previous work showed that OCRed text has a negative cascading effect on natural language processing tasks (Alex et al., 2012; Kolak and Resnik, 2005; Lopresti, 2005; Lopresti, 2008b; Alex et al., 2019) or information retrieval (Gotscharek et al., 2011; Hauser et al., 2007; Lopresti, 2008a; Reynaert, 2008) and those using NLP approaches to historical texts, in particular, have to take care regarding how the error rate of OCR can affect analysis (Ryan Cordell, 2017).This means

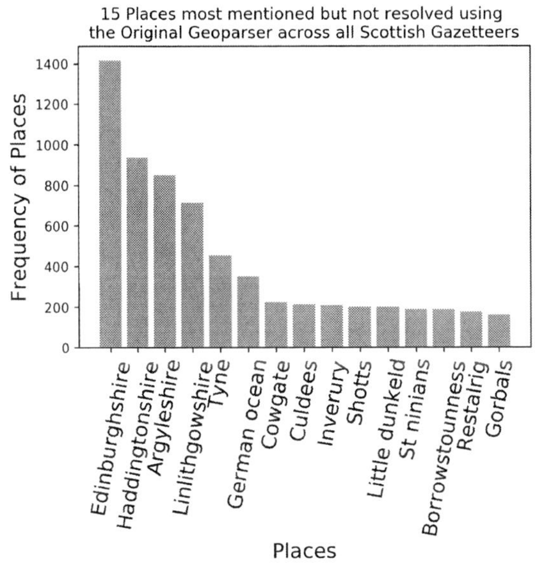

Figure 11: Most frequently identified locations which cannot be resolved with the Edinburgh Geoparser.

that during the evaluation step, we will need to carefully sample from different volumes across the collection to get a balanced view of performance overall. This could involve estimating the quality of the OCR (Alex and Burns, 2014), for example by pages, and selecting samples with different levels of quality.

The Gazetteers of Scotland are descriptive gazetteers with locations often listed alphabetically as opposed to pure alphabetical lists without descriptions. While one would expect that the latter would be easy to tag correctly throughout, for the former type, structure of descriptions can nevertheless be exploited to identify the main names of each entry, especially if the font face or type changes and information is preserved in the OCR. However, this is not the case for place names appearing inside a description as they can often be ambiguous and can overlap with people's names, for example.

Encouraging other scholars to reuse our data will require training in and understanding of these nuances, and it is likely that we will need to run workshops or bespoke support to understand how best to engage with the research communities that this could support (Terras et al., 2017).

6. Summary

We have described our investigations into the flexible deployment of NLP components for automatic and parallel processing of historical text, focusing on the geoparsing of the National Library of Scotland's Gazetteers of Scotland Collection. Our work so far has already made these texts easily searchable both by keyword and by place name grounded to latitude/longitude, but there are several extensions to this work that we wish to take forward. The first is to run the same experiments supplying a bounding box for Scotland to compare results with and without a bounding box. Then, we plan to create a representative annotated test set not only to formally evaluate the performance of various configurations of components but also to determine where improvements to the processing can most fruitfully be made. When complete, this test set can be shared with other research groups who want to evaluate their own geoparsing tools on it. A third strand of future work will be to develop map-based and other data visualisations and to consider how best to provide interfaces to a variety of potential users working within the data carpentries framework, and with the digital humanities community, to establish best practice in data sharing, training, and support structures. Our ultimate goal is to create a digital Scotland-focused historical gazetteer which can be used to drive accurate geotagging and georesolution of other Scottish historical text collections, which we aim to publish openly, for others to use. This would mean that researchers working with Scottish historical text would have the means to interrogate their data by place name and be provided with automatic links to the relevant entries in the Scottish Gazetteers. We are also developing a Text and Data Mining Library Carpentries course to teach researchers how to run different types of text analysis and how to visualise the output.[16]

7. Acknowledgements

This work was funded by the Data Driven Innovation Programme as part of the Edinburgh and South East Scotland City Region Deal. The authors wish to thank Mike Bennett at the University of Edinburgh Library, who runs and supports the Unlock service, and Sarah Ames at the National Library Scotland, who has provided us with valuable insights on the Scottish Gazetteers.

References

Alex, B. and Burns, J. (2014). Estimating and rating the quality of optically character recognised text. In *Proceedings of the First International Conference on Digital Access to Textual Cultural Heritage*, pages 97–102.

Alex, B., Grover, C., Klein, E., and Tobin, R. (2012). Digitised Historical Text: Does it have to be mediOCRe? In *Proceedings of KONVENS 2012 (LThist 2012 workshop)*, pages 401–409.

Alex, B., Byrne, K., Grover, C., and Tobin, R. (2015). Adapting the Edinburgh Geoparser for Historical Georeferencing. *International Journal for Humanities and Arts Computing*, 9(1):15–35.

Alex, B., Grover, C., Tobin, R., and Oberlander, J. (2019). Geoparsing historical and contemporary literary text set in the City of Edinburgh. *Language Resources and Evaluation*, 53(4):651–675.

Borin, L., Dannélls, D., and Olsson, L.-J. (2014). Geographic visualization of place names in Swedish literary texts. *Literary and Linguistic Computing*, 29(3):400–404, 05.

Clifford, J., Alex, B., Coates, C., Klein, E., and Watson, A. (2016). Geoparsing history: Locating commodities in ten million pages of nineteenth-century sources. *Historical Methods: A Journal of Quantitative and Interdisciplinary History*, 49(3):115–131.

[16] http://librarycarpentry.org/lc-tdm/

Filgueira, R., Jackson, M., Terras, M., Beavan, D., Roubickov, A., Hobson, T., Ardanuy, M., Colavizza, G., Krause, A., Hetherington, J., Hauswedell, T., Nyhan, J., and Ahnert, R. (2019). defoe: A spark-based toolbox for analysing digital historical textual data. In *2019 IEEE 15th International Conference on e-Science (e-Science)*, 09.

Gotscharek, A., Reffle, U., Ringlstetter, C., Schulz, K. U., and Neumann, A. (2011). Towards information retrieval on historical document collections: the role of matching procedures and special lexica. *IJDAR*, 14(2):159–171.

Grover, C. and Tobin, R. (2014). A gazetteer and georeferencing for historical english documents. In *Proceedings of the 8th Workshop on Language Technology for Cultural Heritage, Social Sciences, and Humanities (LaTeCH)*, pages 119–127.

Grover, C., Tobin, R., Byrne, K., Woollard, M., Reid, J., Dunn, S., and Ball, J. (2010). Use of the Edinburgh Geoparser for georeferencing digitized historical collections. *Philosophical Transactions of the Royal Society A*, 368(1925):3875–3889.

Hauser, A., Heller, M., Leiss, E., Schulz, K. U., and Wanzeck, C. (2007). Information access to historical documents from the Early New High German period. In L. Burnard, et al., editors, *Digital Historical Corpora-Architecture, Annotation, and Retrieval*, Dagstuhl, Germany.

Kolak, O. and Resnik, P. (2005). OCR post-processing for low density languages. In *Proceedings of the conference on Human Language Technology and Empirical Methods in Natural Language Processing*, pages 867–874.

Lopresti, D. (2005). Performance evaluation for text processing of noisy inputs. In *Proceedings of the Symposium on Applied Computing*, pages 759–763.

Lopresti, D. (2008a). Measuring the impact of character recognition errors on downstream text analysis. In B. A. Yanikoglu et al., editors, *Document Recognition and Retrieval*, volume 6815. SPIE.

Lopresti, D. (2008b). Optical character recognition errors and their effects on natural language processing. In *Proceedings of the second workshop on Analytics for Noisy Unstructured Text Data*, pages 9–16.

Moncla, L., Gaio, M., Joliveau, T., and Le Lay, Y.-F. (2017). Automated geoparsing of Paris street names in 19th century novels. In *Proceedings of the 1st ACM SIGSPATIAL Workshop on Geospatial Humanities*.

Porter, C., Atkinson, P., and Gregory, I. N. (2018). Space and time in 100 million words: Health and disease in a nineteenth-century newspaper. *International Journal of Humanities and Arts Computing*, 12(2):196–216.

Rayson, P., Reinhold, A., Butler, J., Donaldson, C., Gregory, I., and Taylor, J. (2017). A deeply annotated testbed for geographical text analysis: the corpus of Lake District writing. In *Proceedings of the 1st ACM SIGSPATIAL Workshop on Geospatial Humanities*, pages 9–15. ACM.

Reynaert, M. (2008). Non-interactive OCR post-correction for giga-scale digitization projects. In *Proceedings of the 9th international conference on Computational Linguistics and Intelligent Text Processing*, pages 617–630.

Rupp, C., Rayson, P., Baron, A., Donaldson, C., Gregory, I., Hardie, A., and Murrieta-Flores, P. (2013). Customising geoparsing and georeferencing for historical texts. In *2013 IEEE International Conference on Big Data*, pages 59–62. IEEE.

Ryan Cordell. (2017). Q i-jtb the Raven': Taking Dirty OCR Seriously. `http://ryancordell.org/research/qijtb-the-raven/`. Book History 20 (2017), 188-225.

Terras, M., Baker, J., Hetherington, J., Beavan, D., Zaltz Austwick, M., Welsh, A., O'Neill, H., Finley, W., Duke-Williams, O., and Farquhar, A. (2017). Enabling complex analysis of large-scale digital collections: humanities research, high-performance computing, and transforming access to British Library digital collections. *Digital Scholarship in the Humanities*, 33(2):456–466, 05.

Proceedings of he 8th Workshop on Challenges in the Management of Large Corpora, pages 31–39
Language Resources and Evaluation Conference (LREC 2020), Marseille, 11–16 May 2020

The Corpus Query Middleware of Tomorrow – A Proposal for a Hybrid Corpus Query Architecture

Markus Gärtner
Institute for Natural Language Processing
University of Stuttgart
markus.gaertner@ims.uni-stuttgart.de

Abstract

Development of dozens of specialized corpus query systems and languages over the past decades has let to a diverse but also fragmented landscape. Today we are faced with a plethora of query tools that each provide unique features, but which are also not interoperable and often rely on very specific database back-ends or formats for storage. This severely hampers usability both for end users that want to query different corpora and also for corpus designers that wish to provide users with an interface for querying and exploration. We propose a hybrid corpus query architecture as a first step to overcoming this issue. It takes the form of a middleware system between user front-ends and optional database or text indexing solutions as back-ends. At its core is a custom query evaluation engine for index-less processing of corpus queries. With a flexible JSON-LD query protocol the approach allows communication with back-end systems to partially solve queries and offset some of the performance penalties imposed by the custom evaluation engine. This paper outlines the details of our first draft of aforementioned architecture.

Keywords: corpus query system, query language, middleware

1. Introduction

For roughly 30 years specialized corpus query systems (CQSs) have aided researchers in the exploration or evaluation of corpora. During all this time a plethora of different implementations and architectures emerged, with distinctive features or specialization for particular use cases. As corpus resources grow steadily in both size (the number of primary segments such as tokens) and complexity (the number and type of interrelated annotation layers), the need for dedicated query interfaces also became more pronounced.

However, especially the latest generation of CQSs developed during the last decade has revealed an overall decline of expressiveness in their query languages compared to the peak era prior to it. While earlier systems or languages such as FSQ (Kepser, 2003), MonaSearch (Maryns and Kepser, 2009) or LPath+ (Lai and Bird, 2005) offered pretty much the full expressive power of first-order logic, later instances have mostly been limited to the existential fragment (such as ANNIS3 (Krause and Zeldes, 2014), ICARUS (Gärtner et al., 2013) or SETS (Luotolahti et al., 2015)) with only limited support for quantification, negation or closures to cope with the performance issues caused by evaluating complex queries on increasingly larger corpora[1].

Besides obvious scalability reasons, the expressiveness of a CQS can also be a direct result of architectural choices, especially the monolithic approach common to many query engines:

Many CQSs today builds on general purpose database solutions (such as relational database management systems (RDBMSs)) or text indexing frameworks and subsequently delegate the actual query evaluation to this back-end system by translating the original user query from the respective corpus query language (CQL). As such the entire software stack and typically also the CQL itself are bound (and limited) to the data model of this back-end system, giving rise to a series of recurring issues. If a query constraint cannot be directly expressed or evaluated in the underlying (database) query language, it typically won't be available in the CQL (Section 3 lists certain exceptions from this trend). Similarly, if a feature or phenomenon is not explicitly encoded in the back-end storage, it often cannot be used for querying. Last but not least the handling of query results (eloquently dubbed the "Achilles heel of corpus query tools" by Mueller (2010)) differs greatly between systems. From flat or keyword-in-context view in COSMAS (Bodmer, 2005) or FSQ to elaborate tree visualizations in ANNIS or ICARUS, CQSs offer a wide variety of result formats or visual result inspection interfaces, but individual solutions are usually limited to a small subset of this diversity.

To overcome these limitations we propose a novel approach for a hybrid corpus query architecture that combines the performance benefits of modern database and text indexing systems with the flexibility of a custom query evaluation engine[2]. It takes the form of a middleware system called ICARUS2 Query Processor (IQP) between query front-ends and corpus storage back-ends. Due to its modular approach it could also serve as a platform for unification between the heterogeneous tangle of corpus query languages. As this is work in progress we mainly intend to sketch the outline of the overall architecture and its technical details, and open up its merits for discussion with other experts in the field.

The remaining part of this paper is structured as follows: We introduce the overall goals and (preliminary) limitations of our approach in Section 2 and contextualize it within the state of the art in Section 3. Section 4 provides an in-depth

[1] Cf. (Kepser, 2004) in the context of FSQ.

[2] We use this term as a substitution for query engines that can perform the entire query evaluation themselves, typically in-memory on a live corpus and index-less.

overview of the different components in the architecture, including example queries to highlight query capabilities. Section 5 contains location and licensing information for the source code and Section 6 concludes.

2. Goals and Limitations

With IQP we aim at solving a rather broad range of issues. The primary goals of our proposed architecture are the following, with certain initial limitations listed afterwards:

1. To provide **unified query endpoint**. That is, a query language and associated protocol for expressing arbitrary information needs against linguistic corpora. This does however not pertain to any form of user interface, as the entire system as described in Section 4 is meant to be embedded as a middleware within an outer infrastructure that provides the graphical means for user interactions.
2. Implementation of a **custom query engine** in the form of a modular, extensible and scalable evaluation engine for queries provided by aforementioned protocol. As hinted at in Section 4.3 the evaluation complexity for queries can easily become exponential in the size of whatever the unit-of-interest (UoI) for the query is. It is therefore difficult to make general performance guarantees and we estimate the overall performance to be several magnitudes behind specialized index-based alternatives. While this might sound prohibitive for large-scale usage, it should be considered a small price to pay for the availability of extended query options.
3. Interfaces to **optional back-ends** to maximally exploit the performance benefits of existing database and test indexing systems. Ideally this can be realized in a black-box design where the middleware itself only needs to be concerned with a series of (service) endpoints to whom preprocessed queries can be forwarded and which return result candidates and information about solved query sub-parts.

While the architecture sketch in Section 4 displays the entire query evaluation workflow, there are a few components and aspects that we do not intend to fully address in the first prototype phase of our middleware, leading to a few (temporary) limitations on the following aspects:

Result preparation While ultimately of great importance in the long run, we initially focus on the query evaluation itself and leave the extended result processing for a later iteration. The query protocol in Section 4.2 contains placeholders for the subsequent declaration of result formats and script-like processing instructions, but basic result settings such as size, sorting or filtering are already part of the initial draft.

Back-end wrappers As back-end systems are optional and the evaluation engine is expected to be able to handle queries without external help, we do not plan to include actual wrappers for back-ends in the early development.

Graph evaluation While the specification for our query language includes structural constraints for graph constructs (cf. Section 4.3.2), the engine will only be able to evaluate sequence and tree constraints in the first prototype, as those two types also correspond to the predominant data structures used in corpus modeling[3].

3. Related Work

For a very detailed overview of existing CQL families and types of CQSs we refer to the recent work of Clematide (2015). In the remainder of this section we only highlight those (types of) CQSs that are most relevant to our proposed approach or which implement a similar concept.

3.1. Custom Query Engines

The concept of implementing a custom query engine is not entirely new. In fact, several successful CQS already feature their very own evaluation engines:
TIGERSearch (König and Lezius, 2000; Lezius, 2002), FSQ and ICARUS all ship with a query engine that can match structural queries in-memory against a treebank. Similarly, PML-TQ (Pajas and Štěpánek, 2009; Štěpánek and Pajas, 2010) allows to switch its RDBMS back-end for an integrated index-less evaluator implemented in Perl, turning it into a custom query engine for local data.
The popular Corpus Workbench with its Corpus Query Processor (CQP) (Christ, 1994; Evert and Hardie, 2011) is representative for the family of CQSs that provide a custom query engine but at the same time also rely on their own indexing to preprocess corpus data in order to improve query performance. As the associated CQLs of the newer systems mentioned above remain quite limited[4] in their expressiveness compared to our proposed ICARUS2 Query Language (IQL) in Section 4.3, we treat those CQSs as equivalent to off-the-shelf database or text indexing solutions for the purpose of our approach.

3.2. Hybrid Solutions

While traditionally many CQSs implemented the *query translation* approach[5], several systems go beyond that and employ a hybrid strategy for query evaluation.
SETS (Luotolahti et al., 2015) and TreeAligner (Lundborg et al., 2007; Marek et al., 2008) build on RDBMSs for storage, but complement it with their own query evaluation. Slightly different, Ghodke and Bird (2012) extend the text indexing and query engine LUCENE[6] with a custom indexing scheme for storing treebank information.
Those approaches lack a broad coverage wrt query expressiveness, but serve as show cases for successfully evaluating very specific (treebank) queries in a highly scalable manner. Consequently, they too are prime candidates for back-ends in the architecture described in Section 4.

[3]While some approaches, such as SALT (the model behind ANNIS), successfully model complete corpora entirely as graphs, the individual components like sentences or syntax annotations naturally form sequence or tree structures.

[4]The PML-TQ system does however offer the most flexible result processing interface we are aware of, which definitely is an inspiring baseline for the future design of a component in IQP with similar roles.

[5]Using general purpose database or indexing solutions to store the corpus data and delegate the entire query evaluation to this back-end by translating it into its native query language.

[6]`https://lucene.apache.org/`

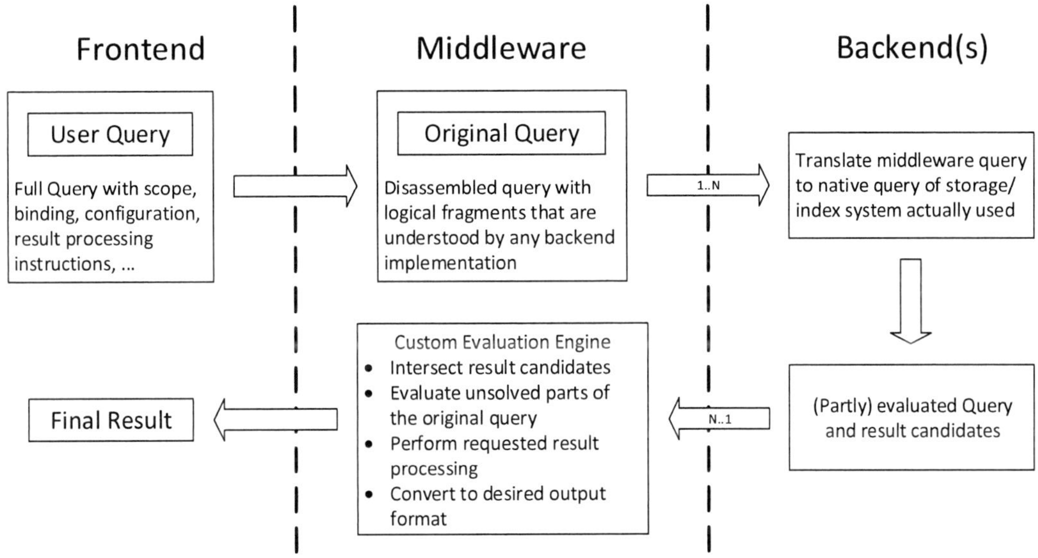

Figure 1: Sketch of the architecture service components and the query data flow.

3.3. Unification & Standardization

Existing efforts on unification or standardization of corpus querying typically focus on the query language level, with notable examples being CQLF[7] (Bański et al., 2016) for a general standardization initiative and KorAP (Bański et al., 2014; Diewald et al., 2016) and CLARIN FCS [8] as actual implementations.

KorAP lets the user choose upfront among several corpora and supported query languages to express a query and then does a N:1 translation into KoralQuery (Bingel and Diewald, 2015), a JSON-LD based query protocol and instantiation of CQLF. The KoralQuery expression is subsequently evaluated by the back-end responsible for the chosen corpus, typically by yet another translation into the respective query language (for the relational database (RDB), LUCENE index or the graph database Neo4j[9]).

On the other hand, the front end of CLARIN FCS provides a single corpus query language with essentially a subset of the expressiveness offered by the individual endpoints that can be queried with it. FCS queries are distributed to different endpoints that participate in the search framework, evaluated locally on each node (akin to a global 1:N translation) and the individual results are then aggregated centrally again and presented to the user.

Both of these approaches improve considerably upon the clutter of (incompatible) corpus query languages and/or evaluation systems. But they also introduce or maintain strong couplings between the front-end (expressed by the CQL or set of CQLs) and the back-end (defined by the actual evaluation engine, typically a RDBMS or similar), and in doing so render it quite difficult to make substantial changes to either.

In the following section we present an architecture that partly resembles KorAP, but introduces an additional fully-independent custom evaluation engine together with a query protocol that completely decouples the traditional front- and back-end roles.

4. Hybrid Architecture

This section describes the proposed architecture for a hybrid corpus query system and its most important components in detail. The overall concept is to decouple features of potential back-end systems and front-end concerns or query language properties. We achieve this by a dedicated middleware layer that mediates between front- and back-end instances and fills feature gaps when it comes to query evaluation or result preparation. Fig. 1 shows this middleware embedded in a typical scenario with a front-end for query construction and result presentation and (optional) back-end(s) with specialized storage and indexing capabilities that allow efficient evaluation of certain query constraints.

4.1. Data Model

IQP build on the ICARUS2 Corpus Modeling Framework (ICMF) (Gärtner and Kuhn, 2018) as its interface to interacting with corpus data. ICMF applies the concept *separation of concerns* to varies aspects of corpus modeling:

Each corpus resource is required to be accompanied by a set of metadata describing its composition, dependencies on other resources, how to access it and optionally providing details on tagsets or other annotation-related information. The data model of ICMF organizes corpora as hier-

[7] **C**orpus **Q**uery **L**ingua **F**ranca. Part of the ISO TC37 SC4 Working Group 6 (ISO/WD 24623-1).

[8] `https://www.clarin.eu/content/content-search`

[9] `http://neo4j.com/`

```
{ "@context" : "http://www.ims.uni-stuttgart.de/icarus/v2/jsonld/iql/query"
"@type" : "iql:Query",
"iql:imports" : [ {
        "@type" : "iql:Import",
        "iql:name" : "common.tagsets.stts"
} ],
"iql:setup" : [ {
        "@type" : "iql:Property",
        "iql:key" : "iql.string.case.off"
} ],
"iql:streams" : [ {
        "@type" : "iql:Stream",
        "iql:corpus" : {
                "@type" : "iql:Corpus",
                "iql:name" : "TIGER v2"
        },
        "iql:rawPayload" : "FIND ADJACENT [pos==stts.ADJ][form==\"test\"]",
        "iql:result" : {
                "@type" : "iql:Result",
                "iql:resultTypes" : [ "kwic" ],
                "iql:limit" : 1000
        }
} ] }
```

Figure 2: A simple mock-up query to illustrate the JSON-LD representation used in the protocol described in Section 4.2. The query searches the TIGER corpus for word pairs that start with an adjective and end in a word with the surface form "test", ignoring case and only returning up to 1000 hits in a KWIC style. The query also features an import statement for the STTS part-of-speech tagset, allowing more controlled expressions inside query constraints.

archical collections of inter-related layers, each with definite responsibilities. One family of layers is strictly used to model the logical and structural composition of a corpus, such as segmentation, hierarchical grouping and relational structures, such as syntax, discourse or coreference in a text corpus. Separated from structural concerns, the actual content (e.g. text, audio or linguistic annotations) is modeled by another layer type acting as mapping from corpus elements to their respective annotations or text content.

This separation of concerns allows the evaluation engine in IQP to also efficiently separate certain aspects of queries and query evaluation: The metadata level provides the basis for binding variables in a query to actual objects in the corpus. It also helps restricting the methods and properties available to expressions inside structural constraints (cf. Section 4.3.2), depending on whether they represent mere sequential structures (such as sentences) or more complex data types, for instance syntax trees. Evaluation of the latter also only needs access to structure-related layers, with the handling of local constraints typically being delegated to subroutines that extract annotation values from the corpus and compare them against those constraints.

4.2. Query Protocol

The architecture overview in Fig. 1 shows multiple (potentially very heterogeneous) service components that need to be able to efficiently communicate with each other during the query evaluation workflow. As such we decided to use JSON[10] as the basic transport format for our query protocol. It is a widely used and lightweight format, and its extension JSON-LD[11] also provides the means for strongly-typed transfer of complex data objects.

Queries in IQP are designed to be self-contained, i.e. they cover the entire information on **which** resource(s) to query, **how** to configure the evaluations engine, the actual query **constraints**, as well as instructions for preparing the **result** returned to the front-end. The following sections provide a brief introduction and examples for some of the main sections in any IQP query[12]. A mock-up query showcasing some of the protocol's features is shown in Fig. 2, parts of which are subsequently used to demonstrate the processing and partial evaluation of query payloads.

4.2.1. Preamble

Each query has a dedicated section that minimally defines the dialect of the query language to be used or defaults to the initial draft version. Beyond that, this preamble section can also contain several optional declarations: **Import** declarations extend the evaluation engine with additional features or modify existing behavior. Simple configuration of the evaluation workflow can be performed via **switches** and **properties**, for instance when disabling case-aware string matching or selecting the direction in which corpus elements should be traversed. Additionally, queries for IQP can embed **binary data** encoded in textual form to be used in query expressions, such as fragments of an audio stream.

[10] JavaScript Object Notation `https://www.json.org`

[11] JSON for Linked Data `https://json-ld.org/`

[12] A more comprehensive specification draft of the query language and the JSON-LD elements used in the protocol can be found online in the working repository (cf. Section 5).

```
1 {
2 "@type" : "iql:Payload",
3 "iql:queryType" : "singleLane",
4 "iql:lanes" : [ {
5   "@type" : "iql:Lane",
6   "iql:laneType" : "sequence",
7   "iql:elements" : [ {
8     "@type" : "iql:Node",
9     "iql:constraint" : {
10      "@type" : "iql:Predicate",
11      "iql:expression" : {
12        "@type" : "iql:Expression",
13        "iql:content" : "pos==stts.ADJ"
14      }
15    }
16   }, {
17    "@type" : "iql:Node",
18    "iql:constraint" : {
19      "@type" : "iql:Predicate",
20      "iql:expression" : {
21        "@type" : "iql:Expression",
22        "iql:content" : "[form==\"test\"]"
23      }
24    }
25  } ],
26  "iql:nodeArrangement" : "adjacent"
27 } ] }
```

Figure 3: Processed version of the payload expression shown in Fig. 2 in line 17. Most notably, the original query expression has been split into two separate node objects with embedded constraint expressions.

4.2.2. Streams

An IQL query contains at least one **stream** definition, typically to extract data from a single corpus. Multiple streams could be used to query for instance parallel corpora or multi-modal data that comprises different sets of primary data with some form of mapping between them. In the initial IQP implementation we will however restrict the engine to only evaluate single-stream queries and leave the extension to multiple streams for a later iteration.

Streams encompass the selection of layers from a corpus to be used, the binding of corpus members to usable variables in query expressions, result preparation instructions and the actual query constraints. Most of those components can be provided to IQP either fully preprocessed or in *raw* statements as described in the following section. Raw statements are automatically compiled during the preprocessing phase of the query evaluation, as described in Section 4.4.

Inside a stream, constraints can be organized in so called lanes, where each lane provides access to a different (concurrent) structural or segmental layer.

4.2.3. Raw and Compiled Statements

When designing a query language and/or protocol, typically a compromise has to be made between succinctness, so that human users can easily write queries, and machine readability or completeness for the processing part. In IQL we support both sides equally:

The parts of a query that carry actual expressions for constraints, sorting or result instructions can be specified both in the form of *raw* statements or compiled objects. Fig. 2 shows an attribute `iql:rawPayload` in line 17 that contains the raw expression used to evaluate results. This is also the minimal form that a human user would have to type in a textual query interface. Subsequent preprocessing during the query evaluation turns this raw form into a more fine-grained separation of objects, visible in Fig. 3. Note how the entire expression has now been divided into nodes, constraints and expressions, that can be individually understood by the evaluation engine or back-end wrappers.

4.2.4. Solved Constraints

Wrappers for the different back-ends used for storage of a corpus are not expected to cover the full range of IQL expressiveness. As such the protocol needs a mechanism to mark already evaluated parts of a query on a very fine-grained level. Any constraint can be marked as `solved` and any element as `consumed`. Fig. 4 exemplifies this on the first node from Fig. 3 (lines 8 to 16). The constraint expression related to the first half of the word pair being an adjective has been marked as `solved` in line 6 with a value of `true` in line 7, meaning that all result candidates returned by the back-end wrapper are guaranteed to contain an adjective at the individually indicated word position. Subsequently, as all of its constraints are solved, the node itself is marked as `consumed` in line 3, allowing the engine to skip its repeated evaluation.

Assuming the back-end was not able to evaluate the second node (lines 17 to 24 in Fig. 3), this situation would now leave the IQP core to only test each candidate for having a word directly following the adjective with a surface form that matches "test" while ignoring case.

```
1 {
2 "@type" : "iql:Node",
3 "iql:consumed" : true,
4 "iql:constraint" : {
5   "@type" : "iql:Predicate",
6   "iql:solved" : true,
7   "iql:solvedAs" : true,
8   "iql:expression" : {
9     "@type" : "iql:Expression",
10    "iql:content" : "pos==stts.ADJ"
11 }}}
```

Figure 4: Example of a solved constraint as part of the answer send from a back-end wrapper to the IQP core.

4.3. Query Language

IQL build on concepts we previously described in Gärtner and Kuhn (2018) and uses a keyword-driven syntax to formulate complex query constraints in a way that is slightly verbose compared to other more compact CQL representatives. It does however provide greatly increased flexibility and basically an integrated scripting language to express constraints.

The two main features of IQL are structural constraints and constraint expressions. The latter can either occur within a structural constraint where they implicitly get access to additional information and methods depending on the type of structure. Alternatively they can be used as global constraints in which case they are limited to bound corpus elements or globally available constants, methods and objects.

4.3.1. Constraint Expressions

Simply put, constraint expressions are arbitrarily complex expressions in IQL that evaluate to a Boolean result[13]. Since a complete introduction to the IQL grammar for expressions is not possible here, we only provide a few examples to highlight certain features. The expressions in Fig. 5 perform the following evaluations: (1) enclosing node is a noun, (2) lemma of enclosing node is one of the three listed movement-related verbs, (3) the bound node is a noun, (4) the parent node of a bound token has at least 5 children in total, (5) the part-of-speech tag of the second-to-last word in the bound sentence does not contain the symbol N (depending on the tagset, this will exclude nouns, proper nouns, conjunctions, past participle verbs and other tags at that position in the sentence).

```
1 pos == "NN"
2 lemma IN {"go","run","crawl"}
3 $token{"pos"} == "NN"
4 $token.parent.size() >= 5
5 $sentence.items[-2]{"pos"} !# "N"
```

Figure 5: Examples of constraint expressions in IQL.

4.3.2. Structural Constraints

Structural constraints define properties that target structures have to meet in order to be considered as result candidates. IQL supports three types of structural constraints, namely sequences, trees and graphs. Their occurrence within a query lane dictates the basic complexity and evaluation strategy for that part of the query, and they also cannot be mixed. In their basic form, structural constraints are always existentially quantified, but by using explicit quantifier statements they can also get existentially negated, universally quantified within their context or marked to occur a specific number of times in a match. Similarly to Section 4.3.1 the following list of examples is not exhaustive and merely intended as a brief overview on some of the structural constraint features available in IQL.

Fig. 6 shows three examples for each of the aforementioned types of structural constraints: (1) is a simple existentially quantified node definition, (2) explicitly quantifies a node to occur at least four times, (3) requires two to five nodes between `$x` and `$y`, (4) is a simple tree with existentially quantified nested child nodes, (5) existentially negates children in a tree node based on some constraint `x`, (6) universally quantifies a child constraint, meaning that all immediate child nodes must satisfy constraint `x`, (7) declares basic graph constraints via nodes and edges, (8) is a negated graph edge, and (9) finally shows the declaration of a explicitly quantified graph edge with its own local constraints.

[13] The specification also defines rules to optionally convert arbitrary primitive values or objects to Boolean values as well.

```
1 []
2 <4+>[]
3 [$x]<2-5>[][$y]
4 [[$x][$y[$z]]]
5 [ ![x]]
6 [ *[x]]
7 [x],[]---[y],[z]
8 []<--![x]
9 <4->[]--[x]->[]
```

Figure 6: Examples of structural constraints in IQL. Note that the angle brackets around numerical quantifiers are optional and only included for readability here.

4.3.3. Example Queries

In this section we demonstrate some of the expressive capabilities of IQL based on a series of information needs of varying complexity defined by Lai and Bird (2004) that have been used repeatedly in other work to compare CQLs and which are listed in Fig. 7.

Q1. Find sentences that include the word "saw".
Q2. Find sentences that do not include the word "saw".
Q3. Find noun phrases whose rightmost child is a noun.
Q4. Find verb phrases that contain a verb immediately followed by a noun phrase that is immediately followed by a prepositional phrase.
Q5. Find the first common ancestor of sequences of a noun phrase followed by a verb phrase.
Q6. Find a noun phrase which dominates a word "dark" that is dominated by an intermediate phrase that bears an L-tone.
Q7. Find an noun phrase dominated by a verb phrase. Return the subtree dominated by that noun phrase only.

Figure 7: Linguistic information needs for querying treebanks defined by Lai and Bird (2004).

The following example queries all assume that the sentence layer has been selected as the primary layer of the query scope and for reasons of simplicity we only show the inner query payloads for most of the examples.

Queries Q1 and Q2 can be expressed in sequence mode:

Q1. `FIND [form=="saw"]`

Q2. `FIND ![form=="saw"]`

From Q3 onward the tree mode can be used and structural constraints are expressed by nested node definitions:

```
Q3. FIND [label=="NP"
          [last && label=="N"]]
```

The `last` keyword is an instruction that forces the engine to only consider the last item within the current context. Without this optimization the constraint could still be expressed by `endsWith(parent)` instead of the `last` keyword, but this would allow the engine to consider and then discard all but the last child during evaluation. Global constraints (used in Q5) provide another efficient way of defining this query by explicitly referencing the last child within the outer node and testing it for being a noun.

Q4. `FIND [label=="VP" ADJACENT [label=="V"][label=="NP"][label=="PP"]]`
With the `ADJACENT` arrangement for a set of nodes the engine will ensure that matches are adjacent[14] to each other in the order they have been declared in the query.
Q5.
```
FIND ADJACENT
    [$np label=="NP"][$vp label=="VP"]
  HAVING ancestor($np,$vp) AS $a
```
Tree matching in IQP is typically performed top-down, which is impractical in cases like this, where bottom-up evaluation is required to find the first node to match the ancestor constraint. Using the `HAVING`[15] keyword, global constraints can be defined which will be evaluated after the basic tree matcher has produced preliminary candidates. A collection of methods modeling tree relations is available to simplify queries such as this one[16]. The query can also be expressed using transitive dominance constraints and explicit (crosswise) negation, but it would (i) be very intricate and (ii) much less efficient to evaluate, as the engine again has to explore many false possibilities.
Q6.
```
WITH $w FROM tokens
    AND $np FROM syntax
    AND $ip FROM intonation FIND
  LANE syntax [$np label=="NP"
      [$w form=="dark"]]
  AND LANE intonation [$ip label=="L"
      && type=="IP" [$w]]
```
This example query contains the entire binding section to illustrate its usage. It also makes use of `LANE` declarations to access information from two different structural layers (here dubbed `syntax` and `intonation` for brevity) and joins them implicitly on the word level. Such a join could also be specified explicitly with global constraints similar to previous examples.
Q7. cannot be expressed fully in the initial IQL draft. As mentioned in Section 2 the specification of result processing instructions is planned for a later iteration. However, since IQL allows very fine-grained control over the referencing of individual parts in a match, restricting the result to only contain selected subparts will be a trivial matter.

4.4. Evaluation Engine

At the very core of IQP sits a custom evaluation engine that manages the preprocessing of queries, delegation to back-end wrappers if available, and most importantly the evaluation of any unsolved query constraints that remain and subsequent result preparation. Relevant parts of the query preprocessing and how (partially) solved constraints and consumed nodes are expressed in the protocol have already been mentioned in Section 4.2. In this section we will primarily and briefly present technical aspects of the evaluation engine that are related to performance and scalability. IQP builds on ICMF and as such uses the in-memory instances of its model during the evaluation process. For every query, a specialized automaton-like *matcher* is created that inspects each unit-of-interest (UoI) in the corpus independently and checks it for being a valid result candidate. In the case of a query focused on syntax, this would normally result in every sentence in the corpus being visited sequentially. Combined with the ability of ICMF to only load selected subparts of a corpus into memory, this enables a highly parallelizable query evaluation: Evaluation on a large corpus can be split over multiple computation nodes, each dealing with a selected region of the entire corpus resource. Within individual computation nodes (or if the engine only runs on a single machine), workload can also be efficiently split across available processor cores, as the evaluation of individual UoIs is independent of each other and so only minimal synchronization overhead is required.
Since this evaluation is performed index-less, the engine is essentially performing an uninformed brute-force search through the entire corpus, which (depending on the type of search and the complexity of query constraints) can potentially cause extremely long waiting times until the query result can be returned[17]. This issue can be offset to a certain degree with corpora being stored in database or text indexing systems with an associated back-end wrapper[18] that can at least handle a subset of IQL and thereby greatly reduce the number of UoIs the engine core has to inspect.

5. Availability

IQP is being developed as a set of Java libraries (requiring a Java 8 runtime environment) as part of the ICMF working repository. The code is freely available under an open source license on GitHub and a comprehensive specification of IQL is also part of the same repository. They all can be found in the general ICARUS2 repository group.[19]

6. Conclusion

In this paper we have presented a hybrid corpus query architecture to address the issue of continued fragmentation in the landscape of corpus query systems and languages. Taking the form of a middleware system between user front-ends and optional database or text indexing solutions as back-ends, it allows to decouple those two traditionally monolithically connected components of CQSs. With its novel corpus query protocol it guides a query evaluation workflow that allows partial solutions from back-ends to be taken into account in order to improve performance.

[14] Adjacency between arbitrary items in the ICARUS2 model is defined based on the mapping to their common foundation layer (if available), which typically contains the basic word tokens.

[15] Inspired by the SQL keyword with the same name, that also is used to extend the capabilities of a query beyond the filter operations of a `WHERE` clause (the equivalent of lanes and/or local constraints in IQL), using aggregate values.

[16] The labels $np, $vp and $a enable nodes to be referenced in additional expressions or global constraints and here are expected to have been bound to represent nodes in the constituency tree.

[17] Depending on sorting or other processing steps for the result, a just-in-time delivery of individual result chunks won't be feasible, as the engine might need the entire set of result candidates to be available first before deciding on which of them to actually return and in what order.

[18] If such a utility is not available for a large corpus, evaluation time could in fact be a prohibitive factor against the usage of IQP.

[19] The metadata behind this persistent identifier leads to both the repository and project pages: http://hdl.handle.net/11022/1007-0000-0007-C636-D

The current reference implementation is programmed in Java and strongly relies on ICMF for corpus interaction. The overall architecture, the query protocol and workflow however are not as strictly coupled to either of those two and as such the entire concept could also be transferred to other technology stacks.

Bibliographical References

Bański, P., Bingel, J., Diewald, N., Frick, E., Hanl, M., Kupietz, M., Pęzik, P., Schnober, C., and Witt, A. (2014). KorAP: The new corpus analysis platform at ids mannheim. Human language technology challenges for computer science and linguistics. 6th language & technology conference december 7-9, 2013, Poznań, Poland, pages 586 – 587, Poznań. Uniwersytet im. Adama Mickiewicza w Poznaniu.

Bański, P., Frick, E., and Witt, A. (2016). Corpus query lingua franca (CQLF). In Nicoletta Calzolari (Conference Chair), et al., editors, *Proceedings of the Tenth International Conference on Language Resources and Evaluation (LREC 2016)*, Paris, France, may. European Language Resources Association (ELRA).

Bingel, J. and Diewald, N., (2015). *KoralQuery – A General Corpus Query Protocol*, volume 111, pages 1–5. Linköping University Electronic Press.

Bodmer, F. (2005). Cosmas ii - recherchieren in den korpora des IDS. *Sprachreport : Informationen und Meinungen zur deutschen Sprache*, 21(3):2 – 5.

Christ, O. (1994). A modular and flexible architecture for an integrated corpus query system. In *Proceedings of COMPLEX'94: 3rd Conference on Computational Lexicography and Text Research*, pages 23–32, Budapest.

Clematide, S. (2015). Reflections and a proposal for a query and reporting language for richly annotated multiparallel corpora. In *Proceedings of the Workshop on Innovative Corpus Query and Visualization Tools at NODALIDA 2015, May 11-13, 2015, Vilnius, Lithuania*, number 111, pages 6–16. Linköping University Electronic Press, Linköpings universitet.

Diewald, N., Hanl, M., Margaretha, E., Bingel, J., Kupietz, M., Banski, P., and Witt, A., (2016). *KorAP Architecture – Diving in the Deep Sea of Corpus Data*, pages 3586–3591. European language resources distribution agency.

Evert, S. and Hardie, A. (2011). Twenty-first century Corpus Workbench: Updating a query architecture for the new millennium. In *Proceedings of the Corpus Linguistics 2011 conference*, Birmingham.

Gärtner, M. and Kuhn, J. (2018). A lightweight modeling middleware for corpus processing. In Nicoletta Calzolari (Conference chair), et al., editors, *Proceedings of the Eleventh International Conference on Language Resources and Evaluation (LREC 2018)*, Paris, France, may. European Language Resources Association (ELRA).

Gärtner, M., Thiele, G., Seeker, W., Björkelund, A., and Kuhn, J. (2013). ICARUS – an extensible graphical search tool for dependency treebanks. In *Proceedings of the 51st Annual Meeting of the Association for Computational Linguistics: System Demonstrations*, pages 55–60, Sofia, Bulgaria, August. Association for Computational Linguistics.

Ghodke, S. and Bird, S. (2012). Fangorn: A system for querying very large treebanks. In *COLING 2012: Demonstration Papers*, pages 175–182, Mumbai, India, December.

Gärtner, M. and Kuhn, J. (2018). Making corpus querying ready for the future: Challenges and concepts. In *Proceedings of the 27th International Conference on Computational Linguistics*, KONVENS 2018, Wien, Österreich.

Kepser, S. (2003). Finite structure query: A tool for querying syntactically annotated corpora. In *Proceedings of the Tenth Conference on European Chapter of the Association for Computational Linguistics - Volume 1*, EACL '03, pages 179–186, Stroudsburg, PA, USA. Association for Computational Linguistics.

Kepser, S. (2004). Querying linguistic treebanks with monadic second-order logic in linear time. *Journal of Logic, Language and Information*, 13(4):457–470, Mar.

König, E. and Lezius, W. (2000). A description language for syntactically annotated corpora. In *Proceedings of the 18th Conference on Computational Linguistics - Volume 2*, COLING '00, pages 1056–1060, Stroudsburg, PA, USA. Association for Computational Linguistics.

Krause, T. and Zeldes, A. (2014). ANNIS3: A new architecture for generic corpus query and visualization. *Digital Scholarship in the Humanities*.

Lai, C. and Bird, S. (2004). Querying and updating treebanks: A critical survey and requirements analysis. In *In Proceedings of the Australasian Language Technology Workshop*, pages 139–146.

Lai, C. and Bird, S., (2005). *LPath+: A First-Order Complete Language for Linguistic Tree Query*. ACL Anthology, 12.

Lezius, W. (2002). *Ein Suchwerkzeug für syntaktisch annotierte Textkorpora*. Ph.D. thesis, IMS, University of Stuttgart. Arbeitspapiere des Instituts für Maschinelle Sprachverarbeitung (AIMS), volume 8, number 4.

Lundborg, J., Marek, T., and Volk, M. (2007). Using the Stockholm TreeAligner. In *6th Workshop on Treebanks and Linguistic Theories*.

Luotolahti, J., Kanerva, J., Pyysalo, S., and Ginter, F. (2015). SETS: Scalable and efficient tree search in dependency graphs. In *Proceedings of the 2015 Conference of the North American Chapter of the Association for Computational Linguistics: Demonstrations*, pages 51–55, Denver, Colorado, June. Association for Computational Linguistics.

Marek, T., Lundborg, J., and Volk, M. (2008). Extending the TIGER query language with universal quantification. In *KONVENS 2008: 9. Konferenz zur Verarbeitung natürlicher Sprache*, pages 5–17, October.

Maryns, H. and Kepser, S. (2009). Monasearch – a tool for querying linguistic treebanks. In *Proceedings of TLT 2009*, Groningen.

Mueller, M. (2010). Towards a digital carrel: A report about corpus query tools.

Pajas, P. and Štěpánek, J. (2009). System for Querying

Syntactically Annotated Corpora. In *ACL-IJCNLP: Software Demonstrations*, pages 33–36, Suntec, Singapore.

Štěpánek, J. and Pajas, P. (2010). Querying diverse treebanks in a uniform way. In Nicoletta Calzolari (Conference Chair), et al., editors, *Proceedings of the Seventh conference on International Language Resources and Evaluation (LREC'10)*, Valletta, Malta, may. European Language Resources Association (ELRA).

Proceedings of he 8th Workshop on Challenges in the Management of Large Corpora, pages 40–46
Language Resources and Evaluation Conference (LREC 2020), Marseille, 11–16 May 2020

Using Full Text Indices for Querying Spoken Language Data

Elena Frick, Thomas Schmidt
Leibniz-Institute for the German Language
R5, 6-13D-68161 Mannheim, Germany
{frick, thomas.schmidt}@ids-mannheim.de

Abstract

As a part of the ZuMult-project, we are currently modelling a backend architecture that should provide query access to corpora from the Archive of Spoken German (AGD) at the Leibniz-Institute for the German Language (IDS). We are exploring how to reuse existing search engine frameworks providing full text indices and allowing to query corpora by one of the corpus query languages (QLs) established and actively used in the corpus research community. For this purpose, we tested MTAS - an open source Lucene-based search engine for querying on text with multilevel annotations. We applied MTAS on three oral corpora stored in the TEI-based ISO standard for transcriptions of spoken language (ISO 24624:2016). These corpora differ from the corpus data that MTAS was developed for, because they include interactions with two and more speakers and are enriched, inter alia, with timeline-based annotations. In this contribution, we report our test results and address issues that arise when search frameworks originally developed for querying written corpora are being transferred into the field of spoken language.

Keywords: MTAS, spoken language data, oral corpora, TEI, query

1. Introduction

When talking about large corpora, one would think automatically of text corpora in the size of billions of tokens. In the context of spoken language, however, corpora with only over one million tokens already qualify for this group. The reasons why written and spoken corpora are looked upon from different perspectives regarding the size are foremost the costs of transcribing the audio/visual material. Additionally, there are difficulties in terms of field access and data protection for collecting authentic and spontaneous interaction data – even more so when various interaction types required for representative language research need to be covered (see Kupietz and Schmidt (2015)).

Even if today the need for search engine optimization (to retrieve huge amounts of big data within a reasonable time) is not a paramount concern in the development of spoken language platforms, there are good reasons to address the issue: The question is whether and how the efficient solutions developed to handle large written corpora can be applied for indexing and querying spoken language transcripts in order to provide uniform ways for accessing written and spoken language data. Could high-performance frameworks be adopted to spoken language without complex modifications? Or would it be necessary to rethink the basic concepts and reimplement the whole software from scratch to suit the special features of spoken language?

Our review of the state of the art of corpus platforms shows that some search engines (e.g. ANNIS[1], Sketch Engine[2], CQPWeb[3], BlackLab[4]), developed for querying written corpora, are already actively applied as search environments on multimodal spoken language corpora (see e.g. Spoken BNC2014[5], Spoken Dutch Corpus[6] and ArchiMob corpus[7]). Unfortunately, no publications could be found that discuss the difficulties that arise when search frameworks originally developed for querying written corpora are being transferred into the field of spoken language.

MTAS[8] (Multi-Tier Annotation Search) developed by the KNAW Meertens Institute[9] in Amsterdam is another open source search engine for querying on text with multilevel annotations. As a part of the ZuMult-project[10], we are currently testing this technology for indexing and querying corpora from the Archive of Spoken German[11] (Archiv für Gesprochenes Deutsch, AGD, Stift and Schmidt, 2014) at the Leibniz-Institute for the German Language[12] (IDS). In this contribution, we are sharing our experience in applying MTAS on three corpora stored in the TEI-based ISO standard for transcriptions of spoken language (ISO 24624:2016) and enriched with different kinds of annotations, especially timeline-based annotations.

In what follows, we first give a short description of our project (Section 2) and then present MTAS - the search engine framework that is in the focus of the present study (Section 3). In the remaining sections, we describe our test data (Section 4), evaluation method (Section 5) and results (Section 6), and discuss some challenging aspects involved in creating and searching indexes of *spoken* language corpora. Section 7 includes the conclusions of our research and provides an outlook on possible future developments.

2. Background

ZuMult (Zugänge zu multimodalen Korpora gesprochener Sprache, Access to Multimodal Spoken Language Corpora) is a cooperation project between three research institutes: the AGD in Mannheim, the Hamburg Centre for Language Corpora (Hamburger Zentrum für Sprachkorpora, HZSK) and the Herder-Institute at the University of Leipzig. This

[1] https://corpus-tools.org/annis
[2] https://www.sketchengine.eu
[3] https://corpora.linguistik.uni-erlangen.de/cqpweb
[4] https://inl.github.io/BlackLab
[5] http://corpora.lancs.ac.uk/bnc2014/
[6] https://www.clariah.nl/en/new/news/search-written-and-spoken-dutch-with-opensonar
[7] https://www.spur.uzh.ch/en/departments/research/textgroup/ArchiMob.html
[8] https://textexploration.github.io/mtas/
[9] https://www.meertens.knaw.nl/cms/en/
[10] https://zumult.org/
[11] http://agd.ids-mannheim.de/index.shtml
[12] https://www1.ids-mannheim.de/

project started in 2018 with a twofold purpose: On the one hand, a software architecture for a unified access to spoken language resources located in different repositories should be developed. On the other hand, user-group specific web-based services (e.g. for language teaching research or for discourse and conversation analysis) should be designed and implemented based on this architecture. The concept involves two parallel modules: 1) Object-oriented modeling of spoken language corpus components (audio- and video data, speech event and speaker metadata, transcripts, annotations and additional materials) and their relationships; 2) Providing the search functionality that is fully compatible with typical characteristics of spoken language. While the first module is primarily intended for explorative browsing on the data, the second query module should enable a quick and targeted access to specified parts of transcripts and thus a systematic research in a corpus linguistic approach. Both components are going to be available through a REST API. In this contribution, we focus only on the developments in the second (search) module and describe our work in progress towards selecting a suitable framework for querying spoken language data.

3. MTAS

MTAS (Brouwer et al. 2016) is an approach for creating and searching indexes of language corpora with multi-tier annotations. It was developed to be primarily used in the Nederlab project[13] for querying large collections of digitized texts.

MTAS builds on the existing Apache Lucene approach[14] and extends this by including complex linguistic annotations in the Lucene search index: During tokenization of a document, MTAS handles linguistic structures and span annotations as the same type as textual tokens and stores them on their first token position as Lucene would do this with n-grams. In the Lucene approach, text files to be indexed are stored as *Documents* comprising one or more *Fields*. Each *Document Field* represents the key-value relationship where a key is "content" or one of the metadata categories (e.g. author, title) and the value is the term to be indexed (e.g. in case of the category "title", it can be a token or a token sequence from the title of the text). MTAS indexes linguistic annotations and text in the same Lucene *Document Field*. The combination of prefix and postfix is used as a value of every token to distinguish between text and various annotation layers (cf. Table 1). In addition to the Lucene inverted index, MTAS provides forward indices to retrieve linguistic information based on positions and hierarchical relations.

We chose MTAS because it supports parsing of annotated texts in multiple XML-based formats, among others the TEI-based ISO standard for transcriptions of spoken language, which is used for transcripts in the AGD. To map data with custom annotations to the MTAS index structure only requires adjusting the parser configuration file. Many

IDs	Position	Parent	Token (Prefix [] Postfix)
[00001]	[0-43]	[ ]	[annotationBlock][ ]
[00002]	[0-43]	[00001]	[u][ ]
[00003]	[0-16]	[00002]	[seg][ ]
[00004]	[0-16]	[00002]	[seg.speaker][RH_0233]
[00005]	[0-16]	[00002]	[seg.speaker.sex][female]
[00006]	[0-16]	[00002]	[seg.type][contribution]
[00007]	[0]	[00003]	[word][ja]
[00008]	[0]	[00003]	[id][w122]
[00009]	[0]	[00003]	[norm][ja]
[00010]	[0]	[00003]	[lemma][ja]
[00011]	[0]	[00003]	[pos][NGIRR]
[00012]	[1]	[00003]	[pause][ ]
[00013]	[1]	[00003]	[id][p26]
[00014]	[1]	[00003]	[pause.type][micro]
[00015]	[2]	[00003]	[word][ähm]
[00016]	[2]	[00003]	[id][w123]
[00017]	[2]	[00003]	[norm][äh]
[00018]	[2]	[00003]	[lemma][äh]
[00019]	[2]	[00003]	[pos][NGHES]
[00020]	[3]	[00003]	[word][vielen]
[00021]	[3]	[00003]	[id][w124]
[00022]	[3]	[00003]	[norm][vielen]
[00023]	[3]	[00003]	[lemma][viele]
[00024]	[3]	[00003]	[pos][PIAT]

Table 1: List of tokens extracted from the transcript excerpt presented in Figure 1.

different types of annotations (incl. stand-off annotations, hierarchical relations and overlaps) are supported in MTAS and can be queried using the MTAS Corpus Query Language[15] (MTAS CQL) - a modified version of CQP Query Language[16] (CQP QL) introduced by the IMS Open Corpus Workbench[17] (CWB). Moreover, MTAS is a Lucene-base framework, which speaks in favor of scalability. MTAS is implemented in Java and is freely available as open source code[18].

4. Data

For testing MTAS, we selected three spoken language corpora from our archive (cf. Table 2). These are the Research and Teaching Corpus of Spoken German (Forschungs- und Lehrkorpus Gesprochenes Deutsch, FOLK, Schmidt, 2017), the German part of the Comparative Corpus for Spoken Academic Language (Gesprochene Wissenschaftssprache, GeWiss, Fandrych et al. 2017) and the Corpus of Mennonite Low German from North and South America (Mennonitenplautdietsch in Nord- und Südamerika, MEND, Kaufmann, in print). These corpora with a total size of almost 3.5 million transcribed tokens were collected between 1999 and 2019. While FOLK and GeWiss comprise authentic spontaneous interactions in German language with two and more native as well as non-native speakers recorded in various communication situations in Germany and abroad, the MEND corpus contains Plautdietsch translations of English, Spanish and Portuguese sentences recorded in the USA and South America. Extensive metadata for speakers and speech events are provided.

[13] https://www.nederlab.nl/onderzoeksportaal/
[14] https://lucene.apache.org
[15] https://textexploration.github.io/mtas/search_cql.html
[16] http://cwb.sourceforge.net/files/CQP_Tutorial/
[17] http://cwb.sourceforge.net/
[18] https://textexploration.github.io/mtas/download.html

Corpus	Data Type	Recording Time	Size (h)	Transcribed Tokens	Speech Events	Documented Speakers	Annotations
FOLK	interactions, audio, video	2003-2019	250	2429489	306	876	normalized forms, part-of-speech tags, lemmas, phonetic annotations, speech-rate
GeWiss	interactions, audio	2009-2012	92	743402	257	480	normalized forms, part-of-speech tags, lemmas, code-switching incl. translations, discourse comments
MEND	dialect corpus, audio	1999-2002	40	296867	321	322	normalized forms, part-of-speech tags, lemmas, prompt/translations, number of target prompt sentence

Table 2: AGD corpora selected for testing MTAS.

The audio- and video recordings are transcribed in modified orthography ("literarische Umschrift") according to the guidelines for the cGAT minimal transcript (Schmidt et al., 2015). Time-aligned speech segments are tokenized, orthographically normalized and enriched with different kinds of timeline- or transcription-based annotations. The annotations were either performed manually or generated automatically. They include e.g. part-of-speech tags, lemmatization, phonological annotations, speech-rate information, code-switching and discourse comments. The corpora differ according to the annotations they include, but taken together, the selected three corpora cover all types of annotations occurring in the entire corpus archive.

The audio transcripts and annotations are stored in the ZuMult format based on the ISO-TEI standard for transcriptions of spoken language. The ZuMult specification requires the mandatory use of <annotationBlock> elements for grouping utterances[19] of the same speaker and the stand-off annotations referring to them (see Figure 1). <annotationBlock> elements consist of exactly one <u> element containing the basic orthographic transcriptions and may contain an arbitrary number of <spanGrp> elements used to represent annotations of different types. Speaker utterances are fully tokenized and represented as a sequence of word tokens (<w> elements), pauses (<pause>), vocalized but non-lexical phenomena (<vocal>) and non-verbal events (<incident>). All these elements are embedded in <seg> elements directly beneath the <u> element. In our corpora, the <seg> elements correspond to speaker contributions – units of segmentation which are linked in time with the audio signal and which are terminated either by a silence of more than 0.2 seconds or by a change of speaker.

The temporal structure is represented by @start and @end attributes pointing to the @xml:id of <when> elements defined in the timeline. Additional <anchor> elements can be provided inside the <seg> element to specify further time points of interest, e.g. for a detailed representation of speaker overlaps. All elements within <annotationBlock>, except for <anchor> elements, require a unique @xml:id to be addressable for search. All token-based annotations like normalized forms, part-of-speech tags, lemmas etc. are encoded as attributes on the respective <w> element. Alternatively, these token-based annotations as well as all other types of annotations can be presented as spans within a <spanGrp> element. Figure 1 illustrates how transcription-based discourse comments (<spanGrp type ="DK">)[20] and timeline-based speech-rate information (<spanGrp type ="speech-rate">) are represented in our corpora.

5. Method

Before testing MTAS, we conducted an overview analysis of 20 existing search platforms providing access to spoken language corpora (a.o. DGD[21], KonText[22], Spokes[23], CQPweb, OpenSoNaR[24], Corpuscle[25], Glossa[26] and TEITOK[27]). Based on this overview analysis, we collected a set of search use cases and features supported by these platforms, regardless of the use of a query builder or one of the corpus query languages (CQP QL, ANNIS QL etc.) in order to submit queries on spoken language corpora. After that we incorporated the MTAS library into the search component of our corpus access architecture (Batinić et al. 2019) and implemented a simple frontend, in which a corpus can be selected and queries in MTAS CQL can be submitted. Our interest was focused on the following two aspects: 1) whether MTAS can be configured for mapping all types of annotations existing in our spoken language corpora 2) whether we can use MTAS CQL to formulate use cases that we are interested in.

[19] The utterance element (<u>) "is the fundamental unit of organization for a transcription, roughly comparable to a paragraph (<p> element) in a written document. It corresponds to a contiguous stretch of speech of a single speaker." (ISO 24624:2016, p. 6)

[20] "DK" stands for German "Diskurskommentierungen" (=discourse comments)

[21] https://dgd.ids-mannheim.de/dgd/pragdb.dgd_extern.welcome

[22] https://kontext.korpus.cz/

[23] http://spokes.clarin-pl.eu/

[24] https://portal.clarin.nl/node/4195

[25] http://clarino.uib.no/korpuskel/page?page-id=korpuskel-main-page

[26] https://tekstlab.uio.no/glossa2/

[27] http://www.teitok.org/

```
<annotationBlock xml:id="c26" who="RH_0233" start="TLI_67" end="TLI_82">
	<u xml:id="u_d43e2475">
		<seg type="contribution" xml:id="seg_d43e2475">
			<anchor synch="TLI_67"/>
			<w xml:id="w122" norm="ja" lemma="ja" pos="NGIRR" >ja</w>
			<pause xml:id="p26" rend="(.)" type="micro"/>
			<w xml:id="w123" norm="äh" lemma="äh" pos="NGHES">ähm</w>
			<anchor synch="TLI_68"/>
			<w xml:id="w124" norm="vielen" lemma="viele" pos="PIAT">vielen</w>
			<w xml:id="w125" norm="Dank" lemma="Dank" pos="NN">dank</w>
			<w xml:id="w126" norm="für" lemma="für" pos="APPR">für</w>
			<w xml:id="w127" norm="die" lemma="d" pos="ART">die</w>
			<w xml:id="w128" norm="freundliche" lemma="freundlich" pos="ADJA">freundliche</w>
			<w xml:id="w129" norm="Einführung" lemma="Einführung" pos="NN">einführung</w>
			<anchor synch="TLI_69"/>
			<vocal xml:id="b6"><desc rend="°h">short breathe in</desc></vocal>
			<anchor synch="TLI_70"/>
			<w xml:id="w130" norm="äh" lemma="äh" pos="NGHES">ähm</w>
			<anchor synch="TLI_71"/>
			<incident xml:id="n14"><desc>schmatzt</desc></incident>
			<w xml:id="w131" norm="äh" lemma="äh" pos="NGHES">äh</w>
			...
		</seg>
	</u>
	<spanGrp type="DK">
		<span from="w124" to="w129">D2_Anfang</span>
		<span from="w132" to="w141">D1_Thema</span>
		<span from="w142" to="w146">D2_Vorstellung</span>
	</spanGrp>
	<spanGrp type="speech-rate">
		<span from="TLI_68" to="TLI_69">3.44</span>
	</spanGrp>
</annotationBlock>
```

Figure 1: An excerpt of the GeWiss corpus presented in ZuMult format.

6. Results and Discussion

6.1 Indexing

The MTAS configuration file provides a large repertoire of settings allowing us to consistently map our audio transcripts including all types of linguistic annotations to the MTAS search index. This requires no major modifications to the MTAS source code. Still, some difficulties arose because of essential structural differences between written and spoken language corpora.

The main challenge we faced in mapping spoken language data to the MTAS search index was to decide what elements of a transcript (word tokens, pauses, non-verbal sounds, time anchors etc.) can be considered as an equivalent to a text token.

From the point of view of calculating token distances, it would be more appropriate not to consider pauses and other audible and visible non-speech events in the same way as genuine word tokens. But querying these phenomena is very important for many use cases from discourse analysis. Therefore, they should be stored in the search index. Because MTAS does not provide an extra type to parse and index such kinds of annotations, we coded them at the word token level. We did this for <pause>, <vocal> and <incident> elements that are placed between word tokens (<w>) within a <seg> element (see Figure 1).

Furthermore, when talking about word token distances in spoken language, we should consider fillers like "äh" that could occur at any place in a word sequence. Therefore, users have to explicitly specify in their queries if the token sequence may or may not contain such fillers between desired word tokens. In the same way, optional pauses and other non-verbal events may be specified in queries as in (A). Users can be supported by query builders when formulating such complex queries.

(A) [word="herr"]([word="äh"]|<pause/>|<vocal/>|<incident/>)?[pos="NE"]
This query looks for word token "herr" followed by a proper name, where one filler, a pause or another non-verbal phenomenon can occur between "herr" and the proper name

A further general difficulty in querying spoken language corpora stems from the fact that individual tokens are often not synchronized with the audio sound because the audio alignment is usually made in contributions and other units above the word level (mainly due to reasons of efficiency in transcribing). Therefore, the temporal order of any two individual tokens is not always fully determined, and the document order of tokens does not always reflect their temporal order in the recording. This applies when speakers' contributions overlap. It can be exemplified by the transcript excerpt in Figure 2. In the transcription document, the word token "hm" of speaker "HA" in line 0003 is directly preceded by the word token "ne" of speaker "PS" in line 0002. According to the timeline alignment, however, "hm" is preceded by and overlaps with the word token "okay".

0001 **SF** ich fa[ng an]
0002 **PS** [bidde oder] (.) hasch du den erschde text (.) oka[y (.) °h] daran könnt er euch dann orientier[n ne]
0003 **HA** [hm]

Figure 2: An audio transcript excerpt with speaker overlaps.

The same problem arises when dealing with token distances. Although the tokens "okay" and "hm" from the example in Figure 2 overlap, the token distance between these words according to the transcript would be 10, because 9 tokens occur between "okay" and "hm" in the transcript file.

The given problems with the token distance and precedence in spoken language corpora pose a lot of questions, that still remain unanswered and should be discussed beyond individual projects. The main question is whether the word token level is the right one to be a base tokenization/position level for indexing spoken language transcripts. Another question is whether individual speakers should perhaps be indexed separately (in a multiple tokenization model). MTAS for its part as search framework provides a flexible and transparent indexing approach that could serve as a starting point for further experiments with different tokenization models.

With regard to linguistic annotations, our experiments revealed that the MTAS indexing approach is suitable for dealing with

- token-based annotations (e.g. normalized form, lemma, POS)
- transcription-based span annotations that refer to a sequence of tokens coming from one speaker
- timeline-based span annotations that fully overlap with the structures (segments, utterances) placed within the same <annotationBlock>
- annotations coming from different annotation sources like different projects or tools for automatic annotation (e.g. Tree Tagger[28], MATE-Parser[29], OpenNLP[30])

Our intervention was needed for coding timeline-based annotations referring to a part of a segment. In MTAS, the end and the start of such annotations are automatically synchronized with the end and the start of the annotation block they are located in, because – according to the time references – the position of particular annotations cannot be encoded. We reimplemented the MTAS parser to replace time references with IDs of tokens located nearest to the respective time anchor. In that way, we achieved a more precise output, especially when annotations refer to a small part of a very large segment.

Finally, we would like to mention the difference between text and audio transcript with regard to metadata. While speech event information (i.e. information pertaining to the interaction or recording as a whole, such as date of recording, interaction type) is technically comparable with text metadata, speaker metadata (such as sex, age, education, etc.) have to be handled in a special way, because they can refer to discontinuous parts of a transcript rather than to the transcript itself. This applies for corpora consisting of interactions of two and more speakers. By using MTAS, we could easily index speaker information in the same way as structures and span annotations at the first token position of every segment originated from the respective speaker. For a query example, see Example (E).

6.2 Query

Once the MTAS index is created, it can be searched by using MTAS CQL. A closer look at this query language (QL) shows that MTAS CQL differs from all known QLs coming from the CQP family (e.g. Poliqarp[31], Sketch Engine's CQL[32], BlackLab's CQL[33]) and therefore represents yet another CQP dialect. It supports different types of search queries including positional constraints (A, B), containment (C, D) and intersecting relations (E, F). It allows to specify the distance and the precedence relation between query elements (G, H) as well as to use RegEx and Boolean operators for specifying token conditions (D, I).

(A) <seg>([word="vielen"][word="dank"])
This query looks for segments starting with "vielen dank"

(B) [incident="lacht"]</seg>
This query looks for a laughter at the end of a segment

(C) <seg.speaker="SF"/> !containing [lemma="äh"]
This query looks for segments of speaker "SF" not containing any forms of the filler "äh"

(D) [pos=".V.*"] within <DK="D1_Zeit"/>
This query looks for verbs in passages annotated with the tag "D1_Zeit" [34]

(E) <seg.speaker="PS"/> intersecting (<seg.speaker.sex="female"/> containing [lemma="hm"])
This query looks for segments of speaker "PF" intersecting with segments coming from female speakers and containing any forms of "hm"

(F) <seg/> fullyalignedwith ([word="so"]{2})
This query looks for segments consisting of two word tokens "so"

(G) [word="ich"][]{1,3}[word="du"]
This query looks for "ich" and "du" with a minimum of one and maximum of 3 tokens in between

[28] https://www.cis.uni-muenchen.de/~schmid/tools/TreeTagger
[29] https://www.ims.uni-stuttgart.de/forschung/ressourcen/werkzeuge/matetools/
[30] http://opennlp.apache.org/
[31] http://www.nkjp.pl/poliqarp/help/ense3.html
[32] https://www.sketchengine.eu/documentation/cql-basics/
[33] https://github.com/INL/BlackLab/blob/master/core/src/site/markdown/corpus-query-language.md
[34] "D1_Zeit" is a discourse comment used in GeWiss corpus to annotate passages where speakers mention the time limitation of their reports.

(H) [norm="Untersuchung"] precededby [w="die"]
This query looks for all transcribed forms of "Untersuchung" if they are preceded by token "die"

(I) [norm="wir|mir" & !word.type="assimilated"]
This query looks for all transcribed but not assimilated forms of "wir" and "mir"

Our tests revealed certain limitations of MTAS CQL, namely, the absence of some operators that are important for querying use cases typical for the spoken language research, e.g.

- comparison operators "<=" and ">=" that could be used for querying numerical values, e.g. searching pauses or speech-rates shorter or longer than N
- RegEx "*" (0 or more) and "+" (1 or more) that can be used in a token sequence to find e.g. two certain word tokens also if some fillers, pauses and other transcribed phenomena occur in between
- variables that can be used to refer to query elements as implemented in Poliqarp (J) or SketchEngine (K). Such references are important to search for repetitions and speaker overlaps (L).

(J) [case=$1 & pos=adj] [case=$1 & pos=subst]
This query is formulated in Poliqarp and looks for an adjective followed by a noun in case agreement with the preceded adjective

(K) 1:[] 2:[] & 1.word = 2.word
This query is formulated in Sketch Engine's CQL and looks for a word token repetition

(L) (<seg.speaker="$1"/>) intersecting (<seg.speaker="$2"/>) & $1 != $2
This is a fictional query looking for speaker overlaps (= segment A intersecting with segment B whereby both segments contain contributions coming from different speakers)

Our findings were reported to the MTAS developer, and meanwhile, some operators that we missed in MTAS CQL during our tests are already implemented in the current MTAS version (v. 8.4.1.1.).

What should be particularly emphasized is the flexibility of MTAS QL regarding different types of annotations: new annotation levels can be added to transcripts without the need to adapt the QL or to change other settings in the MTAS configuration. Just adding a new <spanGrp> element to the transcript, specifying its @type attribute and reindexing the corpus is sufficient to be able to search for these new annotations. For example, if disfluency annotations are added as shown in (M), queries <disfluency/>, <disfluency="TROUBLE"/> or <disfluency="REPAIR"/> can be used to find the spans corresponding to these annotations.

(M)
```
<spanGrp type="disfluency">
    <span from="w874" to="w875">
        TROUBLE</span>
    <span from="w876" to="w880">
        REPAIR</span>
</spanGrp>
```

6.3 Search Output

Every hit retrieved from the MTAS index contains all tokens occurring at the matched positions. For example, searching for [lemma="äh"] in the index excerpt from Table 1 would return the following list of MTAS tokens:

[annotationBlock][ ], [u][ ], [seg][ ], [seg.speaker][RH_0233], [seg.speaker.sex][female], [seg.type][contribution], [word][ähm], [id][w123], [norm][äh], [lemma][äh], [pos][NGHES]

From this output, token IDs can be extracted and used to find the corresponding place in the appropriate transcript. All structures and linguistic annotations for the match are also available for different representations in the user interface.

The difficulty arises when determining the context of the match, e.g. for the presentation in a KWIC view. Here, we come across the problem that was already mentioned in Section 6.1. The context around words in a transcript document (consisting of a list of speaker contributions) is not necessarily identical to the immediately preceding and following context in the audio. The real context can be determined only if all individual tokens are aligned with the original recording. It is against this background that further questions arise, e.g. what exactly is the context of one word occurring within speaker overlaps? Is KWIC maybe not the optimal output/visualization form for all types of search results in case of spoken language? Even if these issues do not primarily concern MTAS, we find it important to mention them in this paper, because sooner or later, any developer of search platforms for spoken language corpora will be faced with these questions.

7. Conclusion and Future Work

Applying MTAS for indexing and querying corpora described in Section 4 revealed that this framework is suitable to be used as a search environment for AGD corpora in their present state. With MTAS, we achieve a good first approximation to a query mechanism for spoken language corpora which is both sufficiently similar to established query mechanisms for written language, and which can at the same time handle a substantial proportion of the structures and annotations specific to spoken language.

As a next step, we plan to enrich our data by discontinuous annotations, relations and annotations that do not refer to the concrete speaker but to parts of the interaction itself like annotations of sequences of social actions as they are used in the research field of Conversation Analysis (cf. ten Have, 2007). It would be interesting to see how such annotations can be indexed and searched with MTAS. We suspect there will be challenges of two kinds: 1) to find the right form for the presentation of such annotations and this form should suit both the ISO-TEI and the MTAS input format 2) to specify the search output if annotations refer to passages with speaker overlaps.

The clear and structured code of MTAS offers opportunities for further development. We see potential for merging the MTAS indexing component with one of the more advanced Lucene-based search modules, e.g.

Korap[35]. Korap supports Koral QL[36] – a serialization of Corpus Query Language Franca (CQLF, ISO 24623-1:2018) – and therefore provides an extensive set of search possibilities.

The MTAS indexing approach itself has convinced us. It stands out with its extensive parser configuration options. From our point of view, it can be used and is worth a recommendation for indexing spoken language corpora.

8. Acknowledgements

We would like to thank Matthijs Brouwer, the developer of MTAS, for friendly support to better understand the framework. Furthermore, we are very grateful to the anonymous reviewers whose insightful comments helped to improve and clarify this paper.

9. Bibliographical References

Batinic, J., Frick, E., Gasch, J. and Schmidt, T. (2019). Eine Basis-Architektur für den Zugriff auf multimodale Korpora gesprochener Sprache. Digital Humanities im deutschsprachigen Raum, DHd 2019 28.3.2019, Frankfurt.

Brouwer, M., Brugman, H. and Kemps-Snijders, M. (2016). MTAS: A Solr/Lucene based Multi-Tier Annotation Search solution, Selected papers from the CLARIN Annual Conference 2016, Aix-en-Provence.

ISO 24624:2016. Language resource management — Transcription of spoken language.

ISO 24623-1:2018. Language resource management — Corpus query lingua franca (CQLF) — Part 1: Metamodel.

Kupietz, M. and Schmidt, T. (2015). Schriftliche und mündliche Korpora am IDS als Grundlage für die empirische Forschung. In Eichinger, L. M. (Ed.), *Sprachwissenschaft im Fokus. Positionsbestimmungen und Perspektiven*, pp. 297–322 - Berlin/Boston: de Gruyter, 2015. (Jahrbuch des Instituts für Deutsche Sprache 2014).

Schmidt, T., Schütte, W. and Winterscheid, J. (2015). cGAT. Konventionen für das computergestützte Transkribieren in Anlehnung an das Gesprächsanalytische Transkriptionssystem 2 (GAT2). Working paper available at https://ids-pub.bsz-bw.de/frontdoor/deliver/index/docId/4616/file/Schmidt_Schuette_Winterscheid_cGAT_2015.pdf

Stift, U.-M. and Schmidt, T. (2014). Mündliche Korpora am IDS: Vom Deutschen Spracharchiv zur Datenbank für Gesprochenes Deutsch. In Institut für Deutsche Sprache (Eds.), *Ansichten und Einsichten. 50 Jahre Institut für Deutsche Sprache.* Redaktion: Melanie Steinle, Franz Josef Berens, pp. 360–375 - Mannheim: Institut für Deutsche Sprache, 2014.

ten Have, P. (2007). *Doing Conversation Analysis : A Practical Guide.* London: Sage Publications.

10. Language Resource References

Fandrych, C., Meißner, C. and Wallner, F. (2017). Gesprochene Wissenschaftssprache – digital. Verfahren zur Annotation und Analyse mündlicher Korpora. Tübingen. Stauffenburg.

Kaufmann, G. (in print). The World Beyond Verb Clusters: Aspects of the Syntax of Mennonite Low German. In Auer, P., Hinskens, Frans L. und Kerswill, P. (Eds.), *Reihe Studies in Language Variation*. Amsterdam/Philadelphia: John Benjamins.

Schmidt, T. (2017). Construction and Dissemination of a Corpus of Spoken Interaction – Tools and Workflows in the FOLK project. In Kupietz, M. and Geyken, A. (Eds.), *Corpus Linguistic Software Tools, Journal for Language Technology and Computational Linguistics* (JLCL 31/1), pp. 127–154.

[35] https://korap.ids-mannheim.de, source code: https://github.com/KorAP

[36] https://korap.github.io/Koral

Proceedings of he 8th Workshop on Challenges in the Management of Large Corpora, pages 47–51
Language Resources and Evaluation Conference (LREC 2020), Marseille, 11–16 May 2020

Challenges for Making Use of a Large Text Corpus such as the 'AAC – Austrian Academy Corpus' for Digital Literary Studies

Hanno Biber
Austrian Academy of Sciences,
Austrian Centre for Digital Humanities and Cultural Heritage,
Austrian Corpora and Digital Editions
1090 Vienna,
Sonnenfelsgasse 19, 3rd floor
Hanno.Biber@oeaw.ac.at

Abstract

The challenges for making use of a large text corpus such as the AAC-Austrian Academy Corpus for the purposes of digital literary studies will be addressed in this presentation. The research question of how to use a digital text corpus of considerable size for such a specific research purpose is of interest for corpus research in general as it is of interest for digital literary text studies which rely to a large extent on large digital text corpora. The observations of the usage of lexical entities such as words, word forms, multi word units and many other linguistic units determine the way in which texts are being studied and explored. Larger entities have to be taken into account as well, which is why questions of semantic analysis and larger structures come into play. The texts of the AAC-Austrian Academy Corpus which was founded in 2001 are German language texts of historical and cultural significance from the time between 1848 and 1989. The aim of this study is to present possible research questions for corpus-based methodological approaches for the digital study of literary texts and to give examples of early experiments and experiences with making use of a large text corpus for these research purposes.

Keywords: corpus research, corpus-based literary studies, computational philology

1. Introduction to a Challenging Research Question

In this presentation the challenges for making use of a large digital text corpus such as the AAC-Austrian Academy Corpus for the purpose of digital literary studies will be addressed and a brief introduction into possible ways to achieve that will be given.

The research question of how to use a complex digital text corpus of considerable size for such a particular research purpose is of considerable interest for corpus linguistics and for corpus research in general as it is for the fields of digital literary studies and digital philology alike. Text studies and in particular digital literary text studies rely to a very large extent more and more on the existence, the availability and the specific functionalities of large digital text corpora. Being able to investigate – just to mention a very common feature of such electronic resources – lexical units of various kinds and thereby to search for words, word forms, multi word units, collocations, lexical patterns, named entities and many other or similar linguistic structures in various digitalized texts within a corpus framework has considerably changed and determined the way in which texts are being studied and explored, not only by language scholars and literary historians. For particular questions of literary studies also larger linguistic units of such texts have to be taken into account here as well, which is why corpus-related questions of narrative studies and also to some extent of discourse studies could also come into play, but only very few examples will be given here to show the potential of a possible research agenda following the principles of corpus-based digital literary studies.

The AAC-Austrian Academy Corpus was founded in 2001 and the texts of the AAC are German language texts of historical and cultural significance from the period between 1848 and 1989. The time frame and the text frame of these highly valuable digital collections of German language texts from all over the German speaking areas constitute the first two important dimensions of the text corpus and its research approaches which are based upon a variety of different parameters. The language use and the considerable variety of the text production at the times of the historical periods in focus of this text corpus immediately raise many questions of how to build such a representative texts corpus, in which ways it would be related to other similar endeavours of creating linguistic text corpora with lexicographic objectives or questions

regarding a comparison to more balanced corpora of rather basic linguistic objectives.
At the centre of the considerations for the selection process of the texts to be integrated into the Austrian Academy Corpus however, stands the question of cultural and historical significance, which has led to the construction of a text corpus founded upon principles of specific parameters guided by critical historical, linguistic, literary, cultural as well as empirical principles.
Selected literary texts from the AAC are to be used as examples from this text corpus in order to demonstrate the corpus-linguistic possibilities of lexicographic studies of literature. The aim of the presentation is to present the potential of corpus-based methodological approaches for the study of literary texts, of a whole range of literary production of a certain historical period, and in particular for the study of lexical items and linguistic structures in literary texts. The framework of the AAC-Austrian Academy Corpus offers research options for such corpus-based literary studies. Examples of this research and its potential for corpus-based text studies will be given.

2. The AAC-Austrian Academy Corpus as a Large Text Corpus

Figure 1: AAC-Poster (copyright H. Biber).

The AAC-Austrian Academy Corpus is a large text corpus of around 600 million tokens. It consists of a large variety of different texts predominantly in German language from the period between 1848 until 1989 with a strong emphasis on the first half of the 20th century. The AAC functions as a text research institution and as an example of an experimental corpus that is designed for use in scholarly textual studies. It has been founded in 2001 and most of its textual resources were created in the first decade of the 21st century. The selection of texts to be part of this large text corpus has been based upon a variety of parameters. As the main purpose of the construction of this text corpus has been a primarily lexicographic, or to be more precise text-lexicographic one, the sources of the AAC stem from a variety of different sociological fields and linguistic domains thereby reflecting not only linguistic and literary but also historical and cultural processes. The AAC provides "a highly developed computational infrastructure in order to discover, structure and deliver information about the texts themselves as well as about the processes and phenomena to be observed in these sources." (Biber and Breiteneder 2004). Among the sources are more than one hundred full runs of political, cultural or literary journals, such as "Die Schaubühne" and "Die Weltbühne" or "Die Aktion", published in Berlin in the early 20th century, as well as many other similar sources, of which the most famous satirical journal "Die Fackel", published in Vienna by Karl Kraus, constitutes "the core and starting point for future selections of texts". (Biber and Breiteneder 2002). The "AAC aims to include a wide range of text types from various cultural domains. All these texts will be carefully selected as being of key historical significance and as highly culturally relevant." (Biber and Breiteneder 2004). The sub-corpora of magazines is contributing to a high variation of different text-types to be found in this large text corpus, because traditionally journals include also letters, notes, poems, advertisements, essays and so on. The AAC includes, apart from the magazines a large section of what is called collections, i.e. text books, almanacs, reading books etc., containing articles from various authors, and also a large number of books of fiction, poetry, popular science, essayistic literature or scholarly publications, and so on. Newspapers are also included to some extent, thereby putting an emphasis to publications or certain months of particular historical importance.
In almost all cases all texts had been scanned with industrial book scanners, so that both the actual images of all the digitalized texts are conserved and accessible when searching for words or annotated content. Then these images have been OCR-read with commercial and highly efficient software, before XML-mark-up has been applied in order to deal with the structural elements describing basic properties of the texts and consequently with the application of linguistic standard annotations (such as STTS PoS-tagging for example) as well as on top of that providing layers of more specific semantic or literary types of annotation, for example in the field of named entities like toponyms or personal names and the like, depending on the research efforts possible.
Several digital editions and text corpus tools have been developed within the AAC for the purpose of detailed

investigations of large amounts of literary texts. In order to be able to explore digital text corpora and to be able to conduct research in the fields of text analysis, several million pages of text are available in this form and have been converted into machine-readable text of more than six hundred million tokens of annotated text. As most of the work started some time ago, newer standards of annotation schemes might have to be applied, funding permitted.

Because the AAC represents such a wide range of different text types from many different domains and genres, it is particularly interesting for the corpus-based study of historical developments by means of looking into the lexicographic and lexical data provided by such a resource, as it can be followed over time. The text corpus includes apart from newspapers, literary journals, novels, dramas, poems, essays, advertisements etc. also travel accounts, cookbooks, pamphlets, political speeches as well as scientific, legal, and religious texts, to name more text types.

The AAC provides a great number of reliable resources for investigations into the linguistic and textual properties of these texts, of which not only the literary ones are well selected with consideration and do by no means follow an opportunistic pattern of selection. The intention has from the very beginning been "to digitally present a wide selection of different sources of scholarly, literary, journalistic, scientific, political texts which exercised considerable influence." (Biber and Breiteneder 2004). This text corpus and its methodological approach of text selection gives scholars who are making use of this text corpus a reliable resource to conduct their research. In the following some examples of first experiments and thorough explorations will be given. An overview of the AAC-Austrian Academy has been given in the second "CMLC" workshop (cf. Biber and Breiteneder 2014).

3. Examples, Experiments and Explorations of Digital Literary Text Studies performed within the AAC

The methodological approaches of the AAC-Austrian Academy Corpus are governed by principles of philological exactness, clear efforts in the structuring of texts, systematic and standardized annotation, specific editorial techniques, lexicographic indexing, scholarly commenting, and so on. Therefore the texts are to be made accessible for research efforts in corpus linguistics and digital philology alike. Examples of experimental explorations into the potential of such a text corpus approach can help to describe the scope and possible directions, leading to digital editions, corpus-based dictionaries, digital libraries or data collections, and corpus research in a broader sense.

The "AAC-Fackel" (Biber et al. 2007a), the first AAC digital edition coming out of the AAC-Austrian Academy Corpus, is an online edition of the journal "Die Fackel" used by more than 30.000 readers, that offers free access to its 37 volumes, 415 issues, 922 numbers, comprising more than 22.586 pages and six million word forms. It can be regarded as a model, a "Musteredition" (Biber 2015), as it contains a fully searchable database of the entire journal with various indexes, search tools and navigation aids in an innovative and highly functional graphic design interface, in which all pages of the original are available as digital texts and as facsimile images. The satirical journal "Die Fackel" was published by Karl Kraus in Vienna from 1899 until 1936 and was also a model for the literary journal "Der Brenner" published between 1910 and 1954 in Innsbruck by Ludwig von Ficker, which has been made online available as "Brenner online" in cooperation of the AAC with the University of Innsbruck (Biber et al. 2007b). The text of "Der Brenner" consists of 18 volumes and 104 issues, which is just a small segment of the AAC's overall holdings, is about two million running words of carefully corrected text, annotated and provided with additional philological information. Both digital editions are making subsections of the overall corpus holdings available in a way which was determined by combining the advantages of graphic design and corpus-based linguistic exploration for the benefit of scholarly and scientific exploration, with a special emphasis in the study of lexical forms (Biber 2006).

Both exemplary journals, for which exemplary editions have been built, are good examples of culturally and historically significant language use. In particular the satirical texts by the language and social critic Karl Kraus can function as highly interesting focal points into a critical and rather ideological exploration of language change and semantic shifts in language use by analysing the overall corpus and the specific features and contexts of certain lexical items. In the historical period of the AAC "significant changes with remarkable influences on the language and the language use can be observed. The years of the seizure of power of the National Socialists is of specific interest for such language studies, where various documents and significant collocations, lexical items, and figurative linguistic constructions are taken into account." (Biber 2013). "Building a diachronic digital text corpus for historical German language studies of this particular kind is a particularly challenging task for various reasons. First, the technical difficulties of corpus building in dealing with a large historical variety of different text types and genres have to be taken into consideration. Second, the specific historical parameters and the methodological scope of such an investigation has to be taken into account. The German language of the year 1933 is being considered as a historical focal point for which an exemplary corpus-based research methodology for the study of the German language could be developed. The sources of a first exemplary study will cover manifold domains and genres, not only newspapers and political journals and magazines, which will be at the core, but also several other text types representing the historical communicative strategies will be included. Among them are pamphlets, flyers, advertisements, radio programs, political speeches, but also essays and literary texts as well as administrative, scientific or legal texts, just to name a few examples, which are all difficult to collect. The AAC has started to build up a small collection of ephemera in this field." (Biber and Breiteneder 2013). For this direction of investigation into the language of a specific historical period, but also for a general lexicographic study focussing on general literature, the concept of "container" has been suggested for the structuring process of the corpus (cf. Biber and Breiteneder 2012). Also first suggestions have been made in order to visualize findings within the corpus. (Biber and Barbaresi 2016).

It is possible that corpus research methods based upon a multidisciplinary combination of corpus linguistics, lexicography, historical studies and cultural studies be applied to gain insights into the textual representations of historical collections of such importance. A corpus-based approach is considered promising in this respect, because applying methods of corpus linguistics and testing new strategies of the application of these methods in the context of historical language studies can also be used for studies of the use of metaphorical constructions and idiomatic multi-word units, like idioms that can be regarded as prototypical forms of figurative language, which is particularly interesting for literary studies. In order to name other possible studies done within the framework of the AAC, particular uses of idiomatic expressions have been investigated, as have studies of the use of proverbs been based upon results from the text corpus (Biber 2010) or an analysis of specific thematic texts (Biber 2014), or the specific vocabulary of for example "Austerity in the Thirties" (Biber 2013) or studies of figurative language (Biber 2009), and detailed studies of collocations (Biber, Breiteneder and Dobrovolskij 2002) in a certain historical period, as have academic dictionaries and academic text-dictionaries been compiled with the help of the Austrian Academy Corpus. This text corpus is a highly relevant resource for building lexical resources based upon corpus findings as well as for empirical digital literary studies and beyond.

4. Bibliographical References

Biber, H. and Breiteneder, E. (2002): Austrian Academy Corpus: digital resources in textual studies. In: J. Anderson, A. Dunning, M. Fraser (eds.): *Digital Resources for the Humanities 2001–2002. An edited selection of papers.* (Publication 16) London: Office for Humanities Communication, p. 13-18

Biber, H., Breiteneder, E. and Dobrovolskij D. (2002): Corpus-Based Study of Collocations in the AAC. In: A. Braasch, C. Povlsen (Eds.): Euralex Proceedings Vol.1 2002, p. 85-95

Biber, H. and Breiteneder, E. (2004): "The AAC [Austrian Academy Corpus] - An Enterprise to Develop Large Electronic Text Corpora". In: M. L. Lino, M. F. Xavier et al. (Eds.): Proceedings of the 4th International Conference on Language Resources and Evaluation Lissabon 2004. Volume V, Lisbon: ELRA, p. 1803-1806

Biber, H. (2006): Words in "Der Brenner" lexicographic searches in a new scholarly digital edition of the AAC. In: E. Corino, C. Marello, C. Onesti (Eds.): *Atti del XII Congresso Internazionale di Lessicografia*, Torino, 6.-9. 9. 2006, Vol. 1, Torino: Atti, p. 395-398

Biber, H. et al. (Eds.) (2007a): AAC-Austrian Academy Corpus 2007: AAC-Fackel. Online Version: "Die Fackel. Herausgeber: Karl Kraus, Wien 1899-1936". AAC Digital Edition No 1, www.aac.ac.at/fackel

Biber, H. et al. (Eds.) (2007b): AAC-Austrian Academy Corpus (2007) and Brenner-Archiv: Brenner online. Online Version: "Der Brenner. Herausgeber: Ludwig Ficker, Innsbruck 1910-1954", AAC Digital Edition No 2, www.aac.ac.at/brenner

Biber, H. and Breiteneder, E. (2008): Words in Contexts: Digital Editions of Literary Journals in the "AAC - Austrian Academy Corpus". LREC 2008, Marrakech: ELRA, p. 339-342

Biber, H. (2009): Hundreds of Examples of Figurative Language from the AAC-Austrian Academy Corpus. In: J. Barnden, R. Moon, G. Philip, A. Wallington (Eds.): Corpus-Based Approaches to Figurative Language. A Corpus Linguistics 2009 Colloquium, Colloquium Companion, School of Computer Science University of Birmingham, *CSRP-09-01 (Cognitive Science Research Papers)*, July 2009, ISSN 1368-9223, p. 13-20

Biber, H. (2010): Corpus-based Studies of Proverbs and Proverbial Expressions. In: Rui J. B. Soares (Ed.): *Interdisciplinary Colloquium on Proverbs*, ACTAS ICP09, Tavira: AIP, p. 106-110

Biber, H. and Breiteneder, E. (2012): Fivehundredmillionandone Tokens. Loading the AAC Container with Text Resources for Text Studies. In: N. Calzolari et al. (Eds.): Proceedings of the International Conference on Language Resources and Evaluation LREC 2012, Istanbul, 23.-25. 5. 2012. Istanbul: ELRA, p. 1067-1070

Biber, H. and Breiteneder, E. (2013): The German Language of the Year 1933. Building a Diachronic Text Corpus for Historical German Language Studies. In: Center for Digital Research in the Humanities (Ed.): Digital Humanities 2013 Proceedings. Lincoln: University of Nebraska, p. 107-109

Biber, H. (2013): Austerity in the Thirties. German examples of historical figurative language of austerity from the AAC Austrian Academy Corpus. In: Gill Philip, et al. (eds.): Corpus-Based Approaches to Figurative Language. Metaphor and Austerity. School of Computer Science University of Birmingham, *CSRP-13-01 (Cognitive Science Research Papers)*, July 2013, p. 22-24

H. Biber, E. Breiteneder (2014): Text Corpora for Text Studies. About the foundations of the AAC- Austrian Academy Corpus. In: H. Biber, et. al (eds.) (2014): Challenges in the management of large corpora (CMLC-2) LREC 2014 Workshop-Proceedings. Reykjavik: LREC, p. 30-34

Biber, H. (2014): Mountains of Text. Analyzing Alpine Literature from the AAC. In: DH2014, Digital Humanities Proceedings 2014. In: DH2014, Digital Humanities Proceedings 2014. Lausanne: EPFL, p. 447-448

Biber, H. (2015): AAC-Fackel. Das Beispiel einer digitalen Musteredition. In: C. Baum und T. Stäcker (Eds.): *Grenzen und Möglichkeiten der Digital Humanities. Sonderband 1 (2015) der Zeitschrift für digitale Geisteswissenschaften*. DOI 10.17175/sb001_019, www.zfdg.de/sb001_019

Biber, H. and Barbaresi, A. (2016): Extraction and Visualization of Toponyms in Diachronic Text Corpora. In: Digital Humanities 2016 Conference Abstracts, Cracow: Jagiellonian University & Pedagogical University, p. 732-734

5. Language Resource References

AAC - Austrian Academy Corpus (2001).

Proceedings of he 8th Workshop on Challenges in the Management of Large Corpora, pages 52–57
Language Resources and Evaluation Conference (LREC 2020), Marseille, 11–16 May 2020

Czech National Corpus in 2020: Recent Developments and Future Outlook

Michal Křen
Institute of the Czech National Corpus
Faculty of Arts, Charles University
Nám. Jana Palacha 2, 116 38 Prague, Czechia
michal.kren@ff.cuni.cz

Abstract

The paper overviews the state of implementation of the Czech National Corpus (CNC) in all the main areas of its operation: corpus compilation, annotation, application development and user services. As the focus is on the recent development, some of the areas are described in more detail than the others. Close attention is paid to the data collection and, in particular, to the description of web application development. This is not only because CNC has recently seen a significant progress in this area, but also because we believe that end-user web applications shape the way linguists and other scholars think about the language data and about the range of possibilities they offer. This consideration is even more important given the variability of the CNC corpora.

Keywords: language infrastructures; national corpora; corpus compilation; application development; user services

1. Introduction

Czech National Corpus (CNC) is a long-term project that strives for extensive mapping of the Czech language. This effort results mostly in compilation, maintenance and providing public access to a range of various corpora with the aim to offer a diverse, representative, and high-quality data for empirical research mainly in linguistics. An important point here is the continuity of the data collection that enables researchers to carry out longitudinal studies of language development or to study changes of public discourse in different time periods.

Apart from the corpus compilation, CNC is also very active in creating web applications for working with corpora, as well as in providing user support and all kinds of related services integrated into the CNC web portal at http://www.korpus.cz/.

CNC has an established and growing user community of more than 8,000 registered active users from the Czech Republic (ca 76 %) and abroad (ca 24 %). In 2019, there were on average 3,164 user interactions per day. An interaction is understood here as entering a query into one of the CNC web applications; any further work with the query results is not counted in this number, as well as any other interaction with the CNC web portal.

This contribution builds on the paper presented at CMLC 3 (Křen, 2015) and discusses the main CNC achievements since then. It gives an overview of recent developments in the given domains supplemented by an outline of future plans.

2. Corpus Compilation

The most of the CNC corpora can be characterized as traditional, with emphasis on well-defined composition, reliable metadata and high-quality data processing. The following gives an overview of the main data collection areas:

• Contemporary written (printed) Czech is covered by the SYN-series corpora (Hnátková et al., 2014). Every year, the series is updated with ca 150 million running words (i.e. tokens not including punctuation) of fresh data, mostly newspapers and magazines, so its overall size now reaches 4.5 billion running words. In addition, a 100-million representative corpus is selected from the SYN-series data every five years. Starting with SYN2000, there are now four such representative corpora, with the fifth one, SYN2020, to be published by the end of 2020. All these representative corpora contain a large variety of fiction, non-fiction, newspapers and magazines, with detailed bibliographic and register annotation (Cvrček et al., 2016; Křen et al., 2016), and thus continuously map the Czech printed production by covering consecutive time periods.

• Contemporary spoken Czech can be divided into several areas. First and foremost, it is the spontaneous informal conversations that can be considered a CNC flagship in this area. These are covered by two corpus series: the recently released ORAL v1 corpus (Kopřivová et al., 2017; 5.4 million running words) that summarizes many years of data collection and is now surpassed by the new-generation ORTOFON corpus. ORTOFON features a two-tier transcription (orthographic and phonetic), it is designed as a representation of contemporary spontaneous spoken Czech and therefore, it is fully balanced in terms of the main sociolinguistic categories of speakers (Komrsková et al., 2017; 1 million running words). These are complemented by a one-tier ORATOR corpus that covers semi-formal monologues (the first version released in 2019; 580,000 running words). The compatible orthographic tiers of ORTOFON and ORATOR constitute a suitable base for further extension of data collection to another spoken language domains.

• Parallel corpora are represented by InterCorp, a multilingual parallel corpus (Čermák and Rosen, 2012; Rosen and Vavřín, 2012) with Czech texts aligned on sentence level with their translations to or from 40 langages (27 of them lemmatized and/or tagged). The core of the InterCorp consists of manually aligned and proofread fiction, and it is supplemented by collections of automatically processed texts from various domains. InterCorp is updated every year, the total size of aligned texts released in the latest version of InterCorp amounts to 1.73 billion running words.

• Historical Czech: DIAKORP with its current size 3.5 million running words includes texts from the 14th century, with a recent focus on the 19th century (Kučera and Stluka, 2014; Kučera et al., 2019). In the long-term perspective, one of the main goals is to compile a representative monitor corpus of written Czech that would cover the period from the 19th century to the present and enable a systematic study of language change.

• Specialized corpora for specific research topics:

◦ DIALEKT dialectal corpus (Goláňová and Waclawičová, 2019; 100,000 words) with two-tier transcriptions of older dialectal recordings (from the 1960s until the 1980s), as well as newer probes (from 1990s until present).

◦ Koditex corpus created for the conducting a multidimensional analysis of register variation in Czech (Cvrček et al., 2018; Zasina and Komrsková, 2019; 9 million running words). For this reason, the corpus was compiled to be as diverse as possible, and therefore, it includes samples also from domains not covered by CNC (e.g. transcripts of TV discussions).

◦ NET corpus of semi-official internet communication, currently discussion forums and blogs (published in 2019; 41 million words). NET is not meant to be "just another web-crawled corpus", so the emphasis is not on size, but rather on rich metadata and high-quality text processing.

◦ ONLINE corpus of Czech web media and social networks that will be published in spring 2020 with an overall size of several billions of running words. Source data for the ONLINE corpus are provided by the Dataweps company. This cooperation will also make it possible to update the corpus on a daily basis, with the update size estimated at ca 4 million running words a day.

Apart from the CNC-compiled corpora mentioned above, there are also a number of hosted corpora available via the CNC web portal (see section 5 for more details).

3. Annotation

There are two main kinds of linguistic annotation being actively maintained by CNC: morphological tagging and syntactic parsing. For this purpose, CNC mostly adapts language-independent software tools to enhance their accuracy on Czech, and in particular, in the individual language domains. This is why CNC also works on the creation of training data from these domains that will be used to train third-party tools like MorphoDiTa (Straková et al., 2014).

Currently, there is an ongoing effort to develop a uniform tagging scheme that would cover the very different language varieties present in CNC: written Czech, informal spoken Czech, Czech used on the internet (discussion forums, social networks etc.) and Czech of the 19th century. This effort is coordinated with the authors of the MorfFlex CZ morphological dictionary,[1] in order to make the resulting tagging scheme as close to it as possible. The scheme will be first used for processing the SYN2020 corpus and it will remain stable for a couple of years to come.

Syntactic level annotation is – similarly to the morphological one – carried out by adapting the existing language-independent third-party tools for syntactic parsing and their enhancement by various methods (Jelínek, 2014; Jelínek, 2019); this sometimes requires also the creation of small treebanks (Jelínek, 2017). Currently, only the newer representative written Czech corpora are available with syntactic annotation: SYN2015 and the forthcoming SYN2020.

[1] http://hdl.handle.net/11234/1-1673

4. Application Development

The emphasis on empirical methods in linguistics and the development of digital humanities highlight the need of quantitative utilization of the variety and volume of the data using statistical methods. Furthermore, we believe that end-user web applications shape the way linguists think about the language data and about the range of possibilities they offer. This creates significant demands on the development of user-friendly web applications aimed at researchers in the humanities and social sciences that would easily use them as powerful sources of reliable information.

Currently, there are eight such web applications in CNC, three of which have been developed in 2019 (Word at a Glance, Lists, Calc).

• KonText (http://kontext.korpus.cz; Machálek, 2020a): continually developed web-based general-purpose corpus concordancer that supports various corpus types including spoken and parallel corpora. It is built above the data retrieval and indexing libraries of NoSketch Engine including its core library manatee-open (Rychlý, 2007). The main distinctive features of KonText can be divided into three main groups (Machálek, 2020a):

◦ query construction: query syntax highlighting; tag builder widget for interactive selection of individual values designed both for Universal Dependencies (UD) and positional tagsets; advanced query history with an easy overview, filtering, and marking for later reuse;

◦ data selection: interactive creation of subcorpora by "zooming into" the selected parts of a corpus down to the document level which enables easy examination of its contents;

◦ result presentation and manipulation: easy control over all operations on the query result (including their reproducibility and editable processing chain); rendering of dependency syntax trees; visual representation of dialogues with a clear indication of speaker turns and overlaps for spoken corpora.

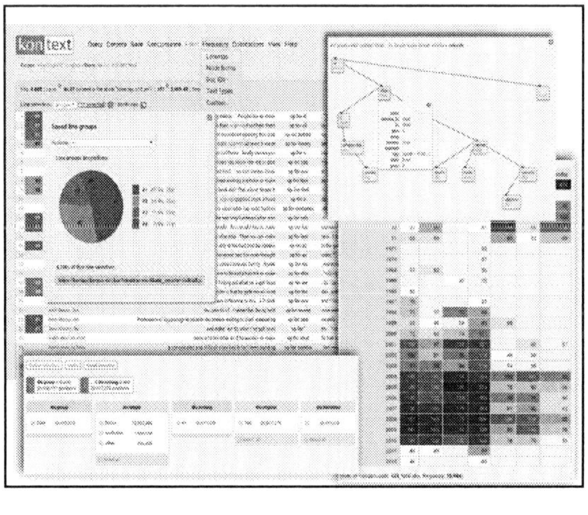

Figure 1: KonText.

In addition, there are many other KonText features not mentioned above, including possible integration with third-party services that may provide additional information about the searched terms. KonText is a mature software developed at GitHub[2] and deployed by some of the CLARIN centres in Europe.

• SyD (http://syd.korpus.cz/; Cvrček and Vondřička, 2011): web application for the corpus-based analysis of language variants. In the synchronic part, frequency distribution and collocations of variants can be compared across different domains of contemporary written and spoken texts, while the diachronic part shows their development over time. SyD provides easily interpretable summarized information with lively visuals and graphics, and it is thus very popular also among the general public.

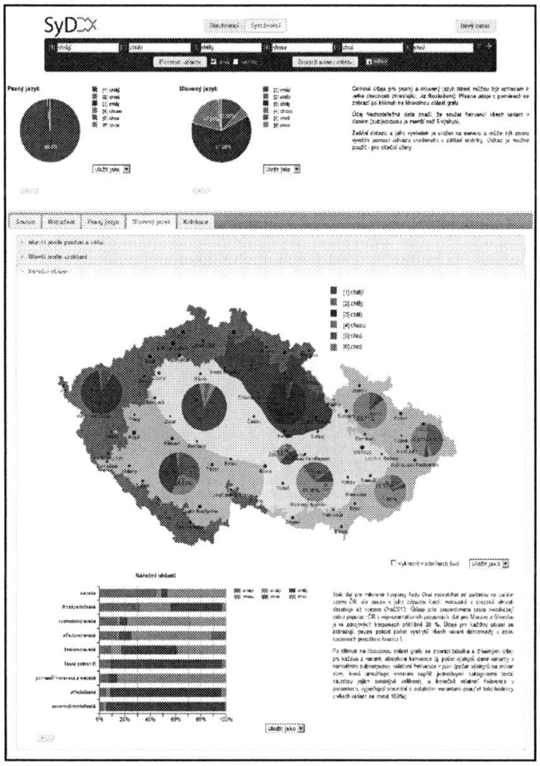

Figure 2: SyD.

• Morfio (http://morfio.korpus.cz/; Cvrček and Vondřička, 2012): web application for the study of word formation and derivational morphology in corpora of contemporary written Czech (extension to other langauges is on the way). Morfio searches the corpus to identify and analyse selected derivational patterns, as specified by prefixes, suffixes or word roots. It can be used to analyse the morphological productivity of affixes and to estimate the accuracy of a selected derivational model. It also includes a list of morphonological alternations.

[2] https://github.com/czcorpus/kontext

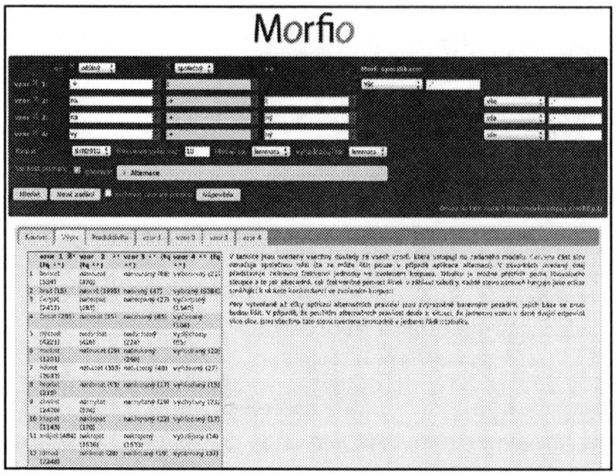

Figure 3: Morfio.

• KWords (http://kwords.korpus.cz/): web application for the identification of keywords (i.e. statistically prominent words usually connected with the text topic) in Czech and English texts. It enables users to upload their own texts to be compared against a reference corpus or a user-selected text. The output is a list of keywords that includes collocations and the keywords are highlighted in the text. KWords also supports the analysis and visualisation of distance-based relations of keywords. It is targeted mainly at scholars and students in text-linguistic and discourse studies.

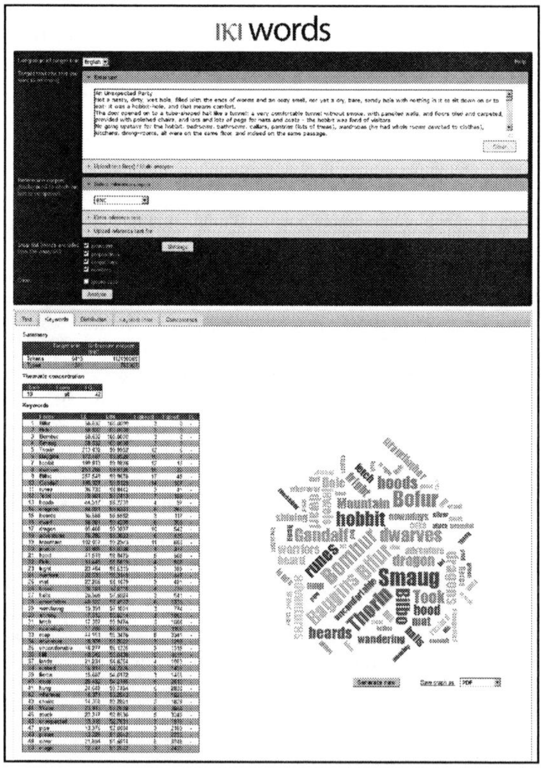

Figure 4: KWords.

• Treq (http://treq.korpus.cz/; Škrabal and Vavřín, 2017): intuitive web interface to automatically-generated translation dictionaries derived from the InterCorp parallel corpus. The users only need to specify their desired language pair for querying either individual word forms or lemmas. The result is a list of translation candidates of the given item sorted by decreasing frequency. By clicking on a particular translation candidate, its occurrences in InterCorp open up in KonText and can be further examined. Similarly to SyD, Treq is very straightforward and easy to use, so it is very popular among students and general public.

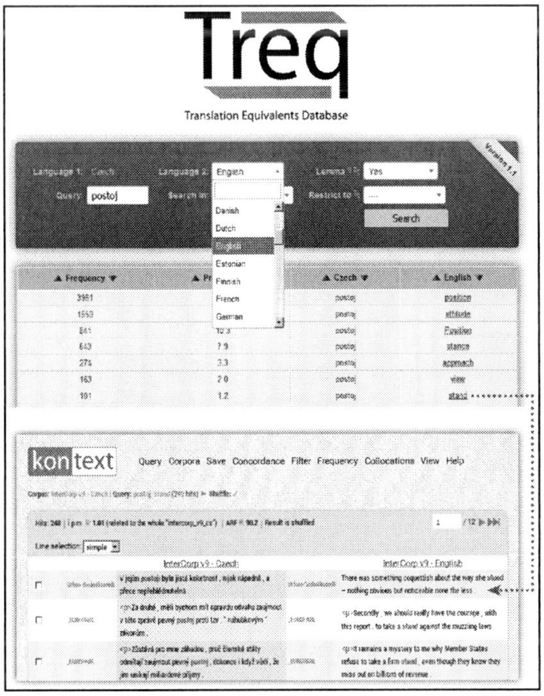

Figure 5: Treq.

• Word at a Glance (https://www.korpus.cz/slovo-v-kostce/; Machálek 2020b) is a brand new web application that has been designed as the main CNC word search service. There are three main operation modes: single word search, two or more words comparison, and word translation mode. In all of them, Word at a Glance (WaG) creates an aggregated word profile that is based on existing language resources (possibly also remote ones) and displayed as a structured and comprehensive overview of various properties of the given word. WaG is an application where many important decisions (which (sub)corpus or statistics to use, its parametrization etc.) have already been made for the user, in order to facilitate (relatively) safe generalizations. Furthermore, WaG has been developed[3] with reusability in mind: deployment and customization by other projects is very easy, adaptation of pre-packaged tiles requires only editing of configuration files.

[3] https://github.com/czcorpus/wdglance

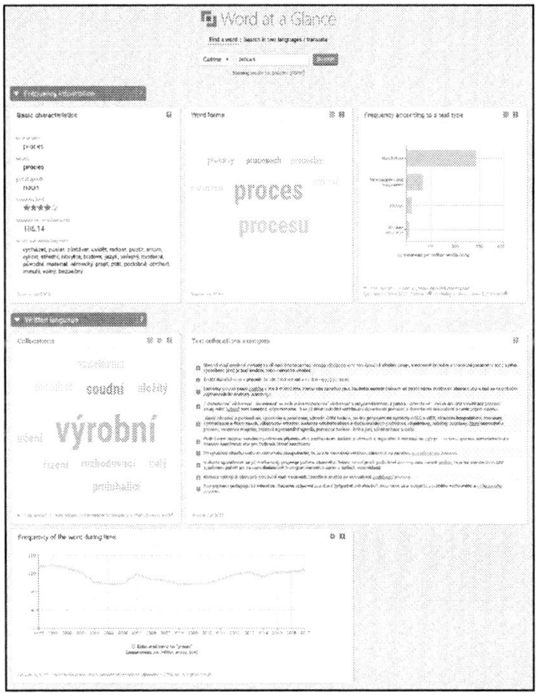

Figure 6: Word at a Glance.

• Lists (https://www.korpus.cz/lists/): simple web application for browsing and comparing frequency lists where they can be inspected, sorted and filtered based on a frequency cut-off, substring and/or part of speech.

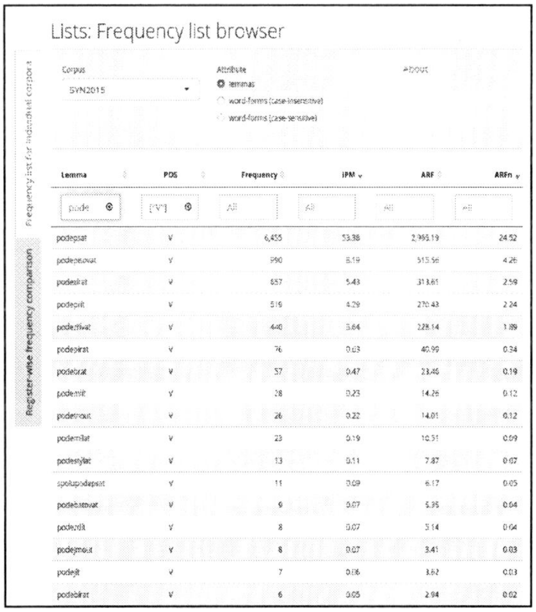

Figure 7: Lists.

• Calc (https://www.korpus.cz/calc/): corpus calculator designed to help the corpus users calculate basic statistical tasks most commonly encountered in corpus research. Currently, there are seven such tasks supported by Calc. Unlike most other statistical calculators, Calc is task-based, which means that appropriate statistical tests are already pre-selected so users don't need to think about their suitability for the given task.

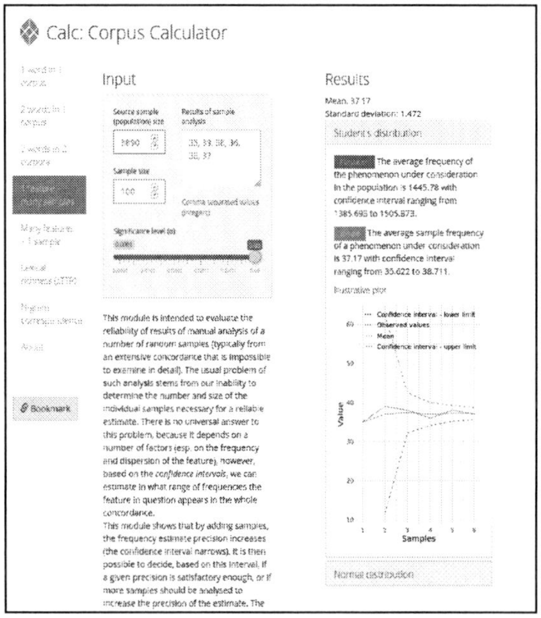

Figure 8: Calc.

5. User Services

User services are concentrated on the CNC research portal at http://www.korpus.cz/ that integrates web applications with user support. The individual services have already been described in more detail in (Křen, 2015) and have been quite stable since then. Therefore, the following overview only summarizes them briefly:

• on-line helpdesk with Q&A that also handles requests for new application features and bug reports;

• web documentation and manuals;

• repository of CNC-based research outputs (currently more than 2,500 entries);

• corpus-based exercises for language teaching at schools;

• corpus hosting (technical processing, quality checks, publication and maintenance of third-party corpora) as a valuable enrichment of the in-house corpora offered by the CNC; currently, the hosted corpora include comparable web corpora of the Aranea series for 14 languages (Benko, 2014), several learner corpora, author corpus of Jan Čep (complemented by the CNC-compiled author corpus of Karel Čapek), Early English Books Online, corpora of Upper and Lower Sorbian etc.

• data packages: corpus-based data sets prepared on demand in case of legal limitations on the redistribution of the original texts;

• consulting, workshops and academic training on various levels.

6. Future Plans

The data collection shall continue along the established lines. As already noted in Section 2, we plan to further extend its coverage to other areas of spoken language, and also to concentrate on building a representative monitor corpus of Czech from the 19th century to the present. However, this goal very much depends on the availability of 20th century texts (until 1989) that are – or at least may be – still subject to the copyright, and thus not generally available from libraries.

As for the annotation, the priority (and also a challenge) is now the development of uniform annotation for all language varieties covered by CNC (cf. Section 3). We are also working on UD annotation of the InterCorp parallel corpus that is currently tagged only by national taggers. The national tagsets usually provide quite rich description in terms of the morphological features covered, but they are not compatible with each other. Therefore, we plan to compile a new version of InterCorp fully annotated in UD (including the syntax), and at the same time, to enhance the UD support in KonText.

The emphasis of the future development of CNC will be put on web applications. In addition to the continuous maintenance and improvement of those mentioned in Section 4, a brand new Map application will be released in 2020. It will display summary information on Czech language dialects on the map, including a description of the individual dialectal features, illustrative corpus-based examples and localization of the corpus probes.

As an output of other project, we are currently building a variation database that records variants (especially stylistic, phonological, orthographic and morphological) of all individual word form and lemma types as evidenced in the CNC corpora. The database will be made available for searching via a dedicated web user interface, and it will also provide valuable paradigmatic information to be added to WaG.

Last but not least, we plan to develop a special application that would examine public discourse based on the data of the ONLINE corpus with its daily updates (cf. Section 2). Its design is still to be discussed, but we believe that it will prove to be a valuable tool for researchers from many domains beyond linguistics.

7. Acknowledgements

The data, tools and services described in this paper are the result of a team work. Many thanks to all for their ideas, hard work and endurance that make the CNC project possible.

This paper resulted from the implementation of the Czech National Corpus project (LM2018137) funded by the Ministry of Education, Youth and Sports of the Czech Republic within the framework of Large Research, Development and Innovation Infrastructures.

8. Bibliographical References

Benko, V. (2014). Aranea: Yet Another Family of (Comparable) Web Corpora. In P. Sojka, A. Horák, I. Kopeček and K. Pala (Eds.), *TSD 2014, LNAI 8655*. Springer, pp. 257–264.

Cvrček, V., Čermáková, A. and Křen, M. (2016). Nová koncepce synchronních korpusů psané češtiny. *Slovo a slovesnost* 77(2): 83–101.

Cvrček, V., Komrsková, Z., Lukeš, D., Poukarová, P., Řehořková, A. and Zasina, A. (2018). From extra- to intratextual characteristics: Charting the space of variation in Czech through MDA. *Corpus Linguistics and Linguistic Theory*, doi:10.1515/cllt-2018-0020.

Cvrček, V. and Vondřička, P. (2011). Výzkum variability v korpusech češtiny. In F. Čermák (Ed.), *Korpusová lingvistika Praha 2011. 2. Výzkum a výstavba korpusů.* Praha: NLN, pp. 184–195.

Cvrček, V. and Vondřička, P. (2012). Nástroj pro slovotvornou analýzu jazykového korpusu. In *Gramatika a korpus 2012*. Hradec Králové: Gaudeamus.

Čermák, F. and Rosen, A. 2012. The case of InterCorp, a multilingual parallel corpus. *International Journal of Corpus Linguistics*, 13 (3): 411–427.

Goláňová, H. and Waclawičová, M. (2019). The DIALEKT corpus and its possibilities. *Jazykovedný časopis* 70(2): 336–344.

Hnátková, M., Křen, M., Procházka, P. and Skoumalová, H. (2014). The SYN-series corpora of written Czech. In *Proceedings of LREC 2014*. Reykjavík: ELRA, pp. 160–164.

Jelínek, T. (2014). Improvements to Dependency Parsing Using Automatic Simplification of Data. In *Proceedings of LREC 2014*. Reykjavík: ELRA, pp. 73–77.

Jelínek, T. (2017). FicTree: a Manually Annotated Treebank of Czech Fiction. In J. Hlaváčová (Ed.), *ITAT 2017: Information Technologies – Applications and Theory*. Praha: Aachen & Charleston, pp. 181–185.

Jelínek, T. (2019). Using a database of multiword expressions in dependency parsing. In K. Ekštein (Ed.), *Text, Speech, and Dialogue. TSD 2019*. Springer, pp. 19–31.

Komrsková, Z., Kopřivová, M., Lukeš, D., Poukarová, P. and Goláňová, H. (2017). New Spoken Corpora of Czech: ORTOFON and DIALEKT. *Jazykovedný časopis*, 68(2): 219–228.

Kopřivová, M., Lukeš, D., Komrsková, Z. and Poukarová, P. (2017). Korpus ORAL: sestavení, lemmatizace a morfologické značkování. *Korpus – Gramatika – Axiologie*, 15: 47–67.

Křen, M. (2015). Recent Developments in the Czech National Corpus. In *Proceedings of the 3rd Workshop on Challenges in the Management of Large Corpora (CMLC-3)*. Mannheim: Institut für Deutsche Sprache, pp. 1–4.

Křen, M., Cvrček, V., Čapka, T., Čermáková, A., Hnátková, M., Chlumská, L., Jelínek, T., Kováříková, D., Petkevič, V., Procházka, P., Skoumalová, H., Škrabal, M., Truneček, P. and Vondřička, P. (2016). SYN2015: Representative Corpus of Contemporary Written Czech. In *Proceedings of LREC 2016*. Portorož: ELRA, pp. 2522–2528.

Kučera, K., Najbrtová, K., Pivoňková, K., Řehořková, A. and Stluka, M. (2019). Korpus českého jazyka 2. poloviny 19. století. *Časopis pro moderní filologii*, 101(1): 92–98.

Kučera, K. and Stluka, M. (2014). Corpus of 19th-century Czech Texts: Problems and Solutions. In *Proceedings of LREC 2014*. Reykjavík: ELRA, pp. 165–168.

Machálek, T. (2020a). KonText: Advanced and Flexible Corpus Query Interface. In *Proceedings of LREC 2020*. Marseille: ELRA. (in press)

Machálek, T. (2020b). Word at a Glance: Modular Word Profile Aggregator. In *Proceedings of LREC 2020*. Marseille: ELRA. (in press)

Rosen, A. and Vavřín, M. (2012). Building a multilingual parallel corpus for human users. In *Proceedings of LREC 2012*. İstanbul: ELRA, pp. 2447–2452.

Rychlý, P. (2007). Manatee/Bonito - A Modular Corpus Manager. In *1st Workshop on Recent Advances in Slavonic Natural Language Processing*. Brno: Masaryk University, pp. 65–70.

Straková, J., Straka, M. and Hajič, J. (2014). Open-Source Tools for Morphology, Lemmatization, POS Tagging and Named Entity Recognition. In *Proceedings of 52nd Annual Meeting of the Association for Computational Linguistics: System Demonstrations*. Baltimore, Maryland: Association for Computational Linguistics, pp. 13–18.

Škrabal, M. and Vavřín, M. (2017). The Translation Equivalents Database (Treq) as a Lexicographer's Aid. In: *Electronic lexicography in the 21st century. Proceedings of eLex 2017 conference*, pp. 124–137.

Zasina, A. and Komrsková, Z. (2019). Koditex – korpus diverzifikovaných textů. *Studie z aplikované lingvistiky*, 10(1): 127–132.

Proceedings of he 8th Workshop on Challenges in the Management of Large Corpora, pages 58–62
Language Resources and Evaluation Conference (LREC 2020), Marseille, 11–16 May 2020

Adding a Syntactic Annotation Level to the Corpus of Contemporary Romanian Language

Andrei Scutelnicu[1,2], Cătălina Mărănduc[1,3], Dan Cristea[1,2]

[1] Faculty of Computer Science, "Alexandru Ioan Cuza" University of Iaşi
[2] Institute of Computer Science of the Romanian Academy, Iaşi branch
[3] "Iorgu Iordan – Al. Rosetti" Institute of Linguistics, Romanian Academy, Bucharest

{andreis, catalina.maranduc, dcristea}@info.uaic.ro

Abstract

In this paper we present an experiment of augmenting the Corpus of Contemporary Romanian Language (CoRoLa) with the syntactic level of annotations, which would allow users to address queries about the syntax of Romanian sentences, in the Universal Dependency model. After a short introduction of CoRoLa, we describe the treebanks used to train the dependency parser, we show the evaluation results and the process of upgrading CoRoLa with the new level of annotations. Out of three variants of parsers trained on manually built treebanks, the one displaying the best accuracy with respect to the recognition of heads and relations was chosen. A number of examples showing types of queries addressing the syntactic level are also presented.

Keywords: syntactic annotation, Romanian treebank, dependency corpus, Universal Dependency, MaltParser, CoRoLa, DeReKo, KoRAP, Poliqarp, DRuKoLa, EuReKo.

1. Introduction

Introducing syntactic annotation in existing corpora is useful for many endeavours: as training data for parsers, as a support layer for addressing syntactic queries to the corpus, as a source for extracting patterns of noun phrases, verb phrases and other types of sub-syntactic compounds, as a complement layer for extracting verb roles, semantic relations, etc. In this paper we describe the process of upgrading the Computational Corpus of Contemporary Romanian Language (CoRoLa[1]) with the syntax level.

At the end of the project, in November 2017, the CoRoLa Corpus had the following parameters:

- almost 400,000 files,
- around 1.26 billion tokens (including punctuation),
- approx. 900 million word occurrences,
- more than 3 million surface unique forms,
- 198,800 words with frequency higher than 50,
- 121,091 lemmas with frequency higher than 50,
- 2,346,546 unique lemma forms, out of which 2,136,391 were lowercase lemmas.

In CoRoLa each document is paired with a metadata file (marking title, authors, year of publication, publishing house, document style, domain, ISBN/ISSN, etc.). The annotations include segmentation to paragraphs, sentences and tokens, while lemmas, POS and morphological features are indicated for each token, and have been obtained with the NLPCube annotator, an end-to-end Natural Language Processing framework (Boroş et al., 2018). Based on recurrent neural networks, the framework[2] performs sentence splitting, tokenization, compound word expansion, lemmatization, tagging and parsing.

The main search frontend of CoRoLa is KorAP (Bański et al. 2012, 2013; Diewald and Margaretha, 2016). Designed and realised at the Leibniz Institute for the German Language[3] since 2011, KorAP, and its user interface Kalamar, were built with the intention to be used as the corpus analysis platform and query frontend for the Reference Corpus of the German Language, DeReKo[4], a corpus that in 2018 counted already 43 billion words (Kupietz et al. 2018). Kalamar's default query language is Poliqarp[5] (Przepiórkowski et al. 2004), which is both powerful for complex annotation queries and easy to use for non-specialists. Being based on regular expressions, Poliqarp allows the user to combine different features in the query, thus exploiting the internal structure of the tags that accompany the primary tokens. Examples are: queries addressing the lexical level, sensible to the orthographical form of (sequences of) words, including endings, prefixes and inner strings of characters, queries addressing the morphological level, regarding lemmas, part of speeches and any combination of features (in both morphosyntactic description tags and category tags), queries exploiting the metadata level, as well as any combinations of these levels. The infrastructure also allows the generation of sub-corpora that observe combinations of search constraints.

Our work is a follow up pursuit of a German-Romanian initiative, the DRuKoLa project[6] (Kupietz et al., 2019), which aimed to create the linguistic data[7] and the

[1] Priority project of the Romanian Academy (RA), realised in collaboration by two institutes of RA: the Research Institute in Artificial Intelligence, in Bucharest, and the Institute of Computer Science, in Iaşi. The query frontend, the project members and a comprehensive list of papers on CoRoLa can be found at http://corola.racai.ro.

[2] https://github.com/adobe/NLP-Cube

[3] *Leibniz-Institut für Deutsche Sprache* (IDS)

[4] *Deutsches Referenzkorpus*

[5] Created in the *Instytut Podstaw Informatyki Polskiej Akademii Nauk* (http://www.ipipan.waw.pl).

[6] A project funded by the Alexander von Humboldt Foundation, which run in the period 2016–2018. DRuKoLa is an acronym from *Deutsch-Rumänische korpuslinguistische Analyse*.

[7] Actually, the Romanian language data, since the German corpus, DeReKo, was running and in continuous development even before 2010, when it counted 4 billion words – according to Kupietz, and Lüngen (2014).

technological basis for performing German-Romanian contrastive linguistics analyses, itself part of a larger international undertaking, having as goal the development of a common platform of comparable corpora, EuReKo (Kupietz et al., 2017).

2. Training the Parsers

We use the MaltParser tool (Nivre et al., 2007; Gómez-Rodríguez and Nivre, 2010) to train the syntactic parser. Three gold treebanks were used during training. The first represents a Romanian translation of a part of George Orwell's novel "1984", with 900 sentences (referred to in the following as the ORWELL set). The annotations, done manually by one of the authors, were in line with the Universal Dependency (UD) conventions[8] (Nivre et al., 2016). The second is a treebank of 9,524 sentences developed at RACAI (Barbu Mititelu et al., 2016), also following the UD conventions (here called the RACAI[9] set). Finally, the third is a treebank developed at UAIC[10], following conventions specific to the Romanian language, which are richer in details than those from UD (Mărănduc and Perez, 2016), out of which we have extracted 8,444 sentences that do not include neither old documents nor chats (we will refer here to this corpus as the UAIC set). Apart from a different set of relations names, other major differences between the two sets of conventions are related to structure and granularity. For instance, relational words in UD are subordinated to the full-semantic word, while in UAIC they are placed above them (see Figure 1[11]). Also, UAIC has 14 types of circumstantial modifiers, while only one type is used in UD.

XML files (Moruz, 2008; Mărănduc et al., 2017) and a script was developed for transforming the gold files from the XML format into the CONLL-U format, used by MaltParser. Then, the MaltParser service was called and its output was converted back into XML, the format supported by both the front-ends and the CoRoLa corpus.
Moreover, a script named Treeops[12] (Mărănduc et al., 2018) was used for transforming the Romanian annotation format into the UD one (mainly by performing surgery operations on the structure, merging more relations into one and renaming relations). Treeops runs error free.
In order to derive training data for the classifier, an oracle is used to reconstruct a valid transition sequence for every dependency structure in the training set. The learning problem in transition-based parsing, as implemented in MaltParser, is to induce a classifier for predicting the next transition, given a feature representation of the current parser configuration. The training is optimised using the LIBLINEAR built-in machine learning package[13].

3. Evaluating the Parsers

Before actually upgrading the corpus on the public server with the new level of annotations, a number of tests were performed locally in order to select the most appropriate training data, to prove the accuracy of the new level of annotation and to test how it responds to queries.
All evaluations were done by using a 10-fold strategy for assessing the accuracy of the dependency parser, actually by comparing its output against parts of the gold corpora. As already shown, we used three different gold corpora, two respecting the UD annotation format (ORWELL and RACAI) and one adopting stipulations specific to the Romanian language (UAIC). We notice as well that, at the moment these experiments were performed, the three mentioned gold corpora we used to train the parser were not yet part of CoRoLa. In principle, at least, there are no major differences between the criteria used in gathering the

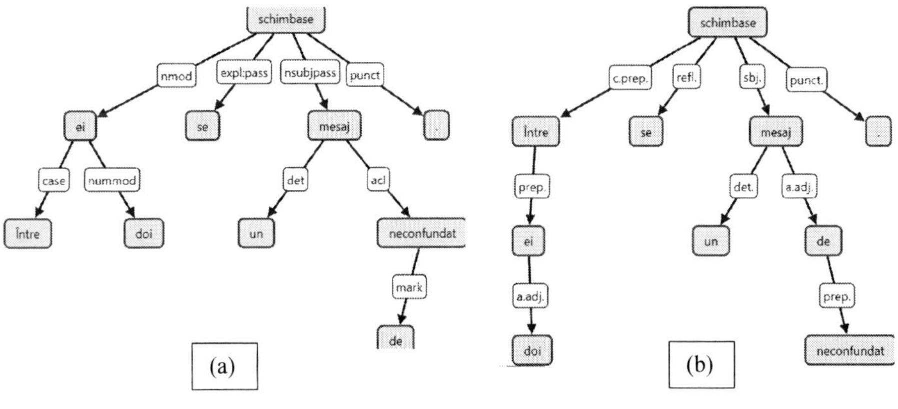

Figure 1: Analysis of the sentence *Între ei doi se schimbase un mesaj de necomfundat.* (*Between them two was exchanged an unmistakable message.* – topic kept). The UD (a) and the UAIC (b) notation of prepositions (*Între* and *de*): they are headed by the semantic word in UD (*ei*, respectively *neconfundat*) and they head the semantic word in UAIC.

Different front-ends have been used to develop these gold treebanks. Sometimes they have been expanded iteratively, using a bootstrapping approach: at each step, an initial corpus, manually annotated, was used to train the parser and then the errors were corrected, producing the next step of the corpus; see details in (Popa, 2010; Perez, 2014). The annotations created by the interfaces are represented as

[8] https://universaldependencies.org/u/overview/syntax.html
[9] Romanian Academy Institute for Artificial Intelligence "Mihai Drăgănescu"
[10] University "Alexandru Ioan Cuza" of Iași
[11] All figures of dependency trees are generated with Treebank Annotator (Mărănduc et al., 2017)
[12] https://ufal.mff.cuni.cz/tlt16/
[13] http://www.maltparser.org/api/index.html

texts for inclusion in CoRoLa, as a corpus of contemporary Romanian, and the texts used for training the parsers, which would hamper to include in CoRoLa also these textual data. Indeed, literary styles, domains, years of writing and other criteria are rather similar, and IPR constraints are also observed, so this will be the next step to proceed.
The accuracy of the parser for different training data is presented in Table 1. The results reported for UAIC refer to the original tag set, not the version mapped to universal dependencies.

The treebank	Head	Relation	Average
ORWELL (UD)	0.896	0.866	0.881
RACAI (UD)	0.642	0.687	0.665
UAIC (non-UD)	0.881	0.910	0.896

Table 1: Accuracy (number of true positives out of the total number of heads or relations) of the dependency parser trained on different gold treebanks. The last column shows the average of the preceding two numbers

We did also a comparison with another dependency parser, which runs as a component of the NLP-Cube, evaluated in CoNLL's "Multilingual Parsing from Raw Text to Universal Dependencies 2018" Shared Task (Boroş et al., 2018). The accuracy of the parser, as reported in the competition, showed lower values than our UAIC-trained parser: for the head – an accuracy of 0.850 and for the syntactic relation – 0.701 (with an average of 0.775).

4. Upgrading the Syntactic Level in CoRoLa

Having these results, it became clear that the best choice for the syntactic annotation of CoRoLa is to use the solution given by the MaltParser tool trained on the non-UD conventions (the UAIC corpus). Let us also note that we can think of two different syntactic annotations of CoRoLa: one following the Romanian conventions and the second – the UD conventions.
To proceed with the addition of this new annotation level in the query platform of the CoRoLa corpus, the steps we must follow are: 1. transposing of already annotated text (token, POS, lemma) from the XML format into the CONLL-U format; 2. parsing the corpus with MaltParser trained on the UAIC treebank; 3. transforming the CONLL-U format that is returned in output by this process back into XML, and 4. converting this format to the one accepted by KoRAP[14], the query platform of the corpus. This pipeline will upgrade CoRoLa with the UAIC syntactic format. To take advantage of the better accuracy of the parser when trained with UAIC data, in order to build the variant following the UD format, a conversion from the UAIC format into the UD format (actually, a simplification) is preferred to the solution of directly adopting a UD-trained parser. The supplementary conversion should be introduced as a step 2', included between steps 2 and 3. Figure 2 shows an extract from the corpus including both UD and UAIC attributes.

```
<S id="1" offset="0">
 <W LEMMA="lui" MSD="Tf-so" POS="DET"
deprel-ud="det" head-ud="1.2" deprel-
uaic="det." head-uaic="1.2"
id="1.1">Lui</W>
 <W LEMMA="Winston" MSD="Np" POS="PROPN"
deprel-ud="iobj" head-ud="1.4" deprel-
uaic="c.i." head-uaic="1.4"
id="1.2">Winston</W>
 <W LEMMA="el" MSD="Pp3-sd--------w"
POS="PRON" deprel-ud="expl" head-ud="1.4"
deprel-uaic="c.i." head-uaic="1.4"
id="1.3">îi</W>
 <W LEMMA="displăcea" MSD="Vmil3s"
POS="VERB" deprel-ud="root" head-ud="1.0"
deprel-uaic="null" head-uaic="1.0"
id="1.4">displăcuse</W>
 <W LEMMA="fată" MSD="Ncfsry" POS="NOUN"
deprel-ud="nsubj" head-ud="1.4" deprel-
uaic="sbj." head-uaic="1.4"
id="1.5">fata</W>
 <W LEMMA="acesta" MSD="Dd3fsr---o"
POS="DET" deprel-ud="det" head-ud="1.5"
deprel-uaic="a.adj." head-uaic="1.5"
id="1.6">asta</W>
...
</S>
```

Figure 2: Concatenation of attributes for head and relation in UD and UAIC notation, for the segment *Lui Winston îi diplăcuse fata asta…* (*Winston had disliked this girl…*)

We are currently working to annotate the whole CoRoLa corpus within the described technology. Thus, the syntax level of CoRoLa will become accessible through KoRAP, in the same way this GUI allows addressing queries referring the syntax level in DeReKo, the German reference corpus.

5. Querying the Syntactic Level of CoRoLa

When this endeavour will be finished, linguists will be able to search remotely for verbal, nominal or other kinds of dependencies, querying the corpus for evidences of language use that touch controversary syntactic issues. Some examples follow.
Studying linearization of attributive adjectives inside the nominal phrase, linguists try to answer the question: is it that sequences of attributive adjectives are strictly ordered, according to a functional projections rule that sees them as cognitive categories (Sproat and Shih, 1988; Cornilescu and Cosma, 2019)?
As shown in Cristea et al. (2019), inventorying types of configurations of syntactic subordinates that a particular word can have is important in the process of elaboration of dictionaries of verbal patterns. As such dictionaries put in evidence typical syntactic-semantic structures for verbs (Levin, 1993; Pană Dindelegan, 1974; Barbu Mititelu,

[14] https://korap.ids-mannheim.de/

2018), they are useful to both linguists and computational linguists. The patterns revealed by searching the corpus could, for instance, be incorporated into a parser as constraints for determining the dependencies associated to particular words.
Another interesting search could be the second-degree dependencies of a word, i.e. the sub-tree linked to a certain word. One example are nested noun dependencies, which are second-degree dependencies that redefine the head (Figure 3).

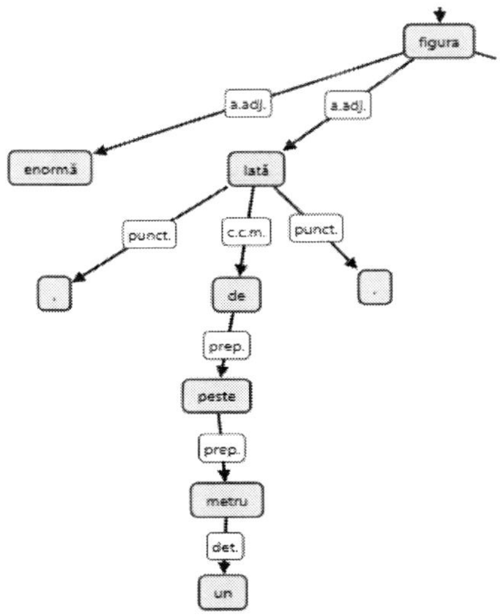

Figure 3: Analyses of the sentence segment: … *enormă, figura, lată de peste un metru,…* (… *enormous, the figure, flat for more than one meter,…*), in which *un metru* (*one meter*) is a sub-constituent of the adjective *lată* (*flat*), and this one – a sub-constituent of *figura* (*the figure*).

Other types of noun dependencies are the appositive dependencies, in which the apposition refers to the same entity as the nominal phrase preceding it. In many types of nominal dependencies, the dependent adds information, narrowing or widening the scope of the head.
A search can be restricted to put in evidence solely elements of the core of the clause (subject, direct or indirect object) or optional elements (adverbial modifiers, nominal modifiers, oblique dependencies). Both situations when the dependencies are expressed by a word or by a clause can be evidenced through a query. Searching the corpus for patterns that relate the complexity of construction of the dependent in correlation with its head can configure parser constraints for future enhancements.
In researches of pragmatic linguistics one can be interested to know the actors involved in a communication act, and the vocative clearly puts in evidence one such direct actor. Here, again, UD conventions differ from UAIC, in UD the words in the vocative case being clearly annotated as belonging to a different syntactic structure.
A whole class of queries and their relevance for linguistic research addressing Romanian syntax is described in (Cristea et al., 2019).

6. Conclusions

The paper presents an experiment of upgrading CoRoLa, the Corpus of Contemporary Romanian Language, with a new level of annotations. To the one already existent, which refers to morphology, the syntactic level will allow users to address queries in terms of heads and dependency relations. Syntax annotation in corpora, following the Universal Dependency model or other models, has been extensively described in the literature. This paper insists on the elaboration strategy of such a level of annotation by making heavy use of the NLP technology. To suggest the degree of applicability of the upgraded corpus, a number of possible queries addressing syntactic dependency structures of Romanian language are also sketched.
There remain many issues to be solved, on which we will concentrate in the near future. First, the technology that we describe here should be made functional on KoRAP, the query infrastructure that supports CoRoLa. Then, we ought to verify to what extend CoRoLa will be now even more useful as an empirical basis for syntactic studies, a question that has been uttered already when CoRoLa had no syntax inside (Cornilescu and Cosma, 2019) and which should be put again now when the corpus is enriched with the dependency syntax, while we are also aware that errors are inherently left behind by the annotation technology. Because of the extremely free word order in Romanian, it is possible for the syntactic head to be separated from some of its dependents by various other subordinates. However, being extremely difficult to parse, with an error rate still high for these long-distance dependencies, we might consider leaving them unparsed. Then the issue is to implement a filtering decision criterion. One possible criterion for this filter could be the computation of a confidence score for a parsed sentence, that would take into consideration individual accuracy scores for different types of relations and the relative word-head distance. The calibration of such a score can easily be done by comparing automatic parses with their equivalents in the gold files.
Finally, we want to keep our promise to augment the corpus itself with the texts used in training.
It is our sincere belief that the addition of this level of annotation will create new opportunities for Romanian language research. Moreover, we hope that the experience described here for the implementation of syntax in this large Romanian corpus could be inspiring for similar endeavours addressing other languages.

7. Acknowledgements

The work described in this paper was performed as part of the research plan of the NLP team in the Institute of Computer Science of the Romanian Academy, Iaşi branch, and was partially supported by a grant of the Ministry of Research and Innovation, Program PN-III-P1-1.2.-PCCDI, nr. 73/2018 - the ReTeRom project.

8. References

Bański, P., Fischer, P. M., Frick, E., Ketzan, E., Kupietz, M., Schnober, C., Schonefeld, O. and Witt, A. (2012). The New IDS Corpus Analysis Platform: Challenges and

Prospects. In N. Calzolari, K. Choukri, T. Declerck, M. Doğan, B. Maegaard, J. Mariani, J. Odijk, S. Piperidis (Eds.), Proceedings of the 8th International Conference on Language Resources and Evaluation (LREC 2012), Istanbul, Turkey, May 2012. European Language Resources Association (ELRA), p. 2905–2911.

Bański, P., Bingel, J., Diewald, N., Frick, E., Hanl, M., Kupietz, M., Pęzik, P., Schnober, C. and Witt, A. (2013). KorAP: the new corpus analysis platform at IDS Mannheim. In Z. Vetulani, H. Uszkoreit (Eds.), Human Language Technologies as a Challenge for Computer Science and Linguistics, Proceedings of the 6th Language and Technology Conference, Poznań, Fundacja Uniwersytetuim. A., p. 586–587.

Barbu Mititelu, V., Ion, R., Simionescu, R., Irimia, E. and Perez, C.-A. (2016). The Romanian Treebank Annotated According to Universal Dependencies. Proceedings of HrTAL2016, Dubrovnik, Croatia, 29 Sept. - 1 Oct.

Barbu Mititelu, A.M. (2018). Valence Dictionary For Romanian Language In Printed Version And Xml Format. In V. Păiş, D. Gîfu, D. Trandabăţ, D. Cristea, D. Tufiş (eds), Proceedings of The 13th International Conference "Linguistic Resources And Tools For Processing The Romanian Language", Iaşi, November 22-23, p. 101–112.

Nivre, J. (2010). Statistical parsing. In Nitin Indurkhya and Fred J. Damerau (Eds.), Handbook of Natural Language Processing. Second Edition, CRC Press, Taylor and Francis Group, p. 237-266.

Boroş, T., Dumitrescu, Ş. and Burtică R. (2018). NLP-Cube: End-to-End Raw Text Processing With Neural Networks. 10.18653/v1/K18-2017.

Cristea, D., Diewald, N., Haja, G., Mărănduc, C., Barbu-Mititelu, V. and Onofrei, M. (2019). How to Find a Shining Needle in the Haystack. Querying CoRoLa: Solutions and Perspectives. In Revue Roumaine de Linguistique, Bucureşti, vol. 64, no. 3, p. 279–292.

Cornilescu, A. and Cosma R. (2019). Linearization of attributive adjectives in Romanian. In Revue Roumaine de Linguistique, Bucureşti, vol. 64, no. 3, p. 307–323.

Diewald, N. and Margaretha, E. (2016), Krill: KorAP search and analysis engine. In M. Kupietz, A. Geyken (Eds.), Corpus Linguistic Software Tools, Journal for language technology and computational linguistics (JLCL) 31 (1), Berlin, GSCL, p. 73–90.

Gómez-Rodríguez, C. and Nivre J. (2010). A transition-based parser for 2-planar dependency structures. In Proceedings of the 48th Annual Meeting of the Association for Computational Linguistics, p. 1492-1501.

Kupietz, M., Cosma, R. and Witt, A. (2019). The Drukola Project. In Revue Roumaine de Linguistique, Bucharest, vol. 64, no. 3., p. 255–263.

Kupietz, M., Witt, A., Bański, P., Tufiş, D., Cristea, D. and Váradi, T. (2017), EuReCo – Joining Forces for a European Reference Corpus as a sustainable base for cross-linguistic research. In P. Bański, M. Kupietz, H. Lüngen, P. Rayson, H. Biber, E. Breiteneder, S. Clematide, J. Mariani, M. Stevenson, T. Sick (Eds.), Proceedings of the Workshop on Challenges in the Management of Large Corpora and Big Data and Natural Language Processing, Mannheim, IDS, p. 15–19.

Kupietz, M. and Lüngen, H. (2014). Recent developments in DeReKo. In N. Calzolari, K. Choukri, T. Declerck, H. Loftsson, B. Maegaard, J. Mariani, A. Moreno, J. Odijk, S. Piperidis (Eds.), Proceedings of the 9th International Conference on Language Resources and Evaluation (LREC 2014), Reykjavik, p. 2378–2385.

Kupietz, M., Lüngen, H., Kamocki, P., and Witt, A. (2018). The German Reference Corpus DeReKo: New Developments – New Opportunities. In N. Calzolari, K. Choukri, C. Cieri, T. Declerck, S. Goggi, K. Hasida, H. Isahara, B. Maegaard, J. Mariani, H. Mazo, A. Moreno, J. Odijk, S. Piperidis, T. Tokunaga (Eds.), Proceedings of the Eleventh International Conference on Language Resources and Evaluation (LREC 2018), Miyazaki, European Language Resources Association (ELRA), p. 4353–4360.

Levin, B. (1993). English Verb Class and Alternations: A Preliminary Investigation, University of Chicago Press.

Mărănduc, M. and Perez, C.-A. (2016). A Resource for the Written Romanian: the UAIC Dependency Treebank. In Proceedings of ConsILR, Mălini, 27-29 Oct., p. 79-90.

Mărănduc, C., Mititelu, C. and Bobicev, V. (2018). Syntactic Semantic Correspondence in Dependency Grammar. In Proceeding of 16th International Workshop on Treebanks and Linguistic Theories Prague, p. 167-180.

Mărănduc, C., Hociung, F., Bobicev, V. (2017). Treebank Annotator for multiple formats and conventions. In Proceedings of the 4th Conference of Mathematical and Computer Science Society of the Republic of Moldova, Chişinău, June 28 – July 2, p. 529-534.

Moruz, A. (2008). Developing a Functional Dependency Grammar (FDG) annotator for Romanian. Master thesis, A. I. Cuza University, Faculty of Computer Science, Iaşi.

Nivre, J., Hall, J., Nilsson, J. and Chanev, A. (2007). MaltParser: A language-independent system for data-driven dependency parsing. Natural Language Engineering, Cambridge University Press, volume 13, p. 95-135.

Nivre, J., de Marneffe, M.C., Ginter, F., Goldberg, Y., Hajic, J., Manning, C.D., Mc Donald R., Petrov, S., Pyysalo, S., Silveira, N., Tsarfaty, R. and Zeman, D. (2016). Universal Dependencies v1: A Multilingual Treebank Collection. In Proceedings of the Tenth International Conference on Language Resources and Evaluation (LREC-2016), European Language Resources Association (ELRA), Portoroz Slovenia, p. 1659–1666.

Pană Dindelegan, G. (1974). Sintaxa transformaţională a grupului verbal în limba română, Bucureşti, Editura Academiei.

Perez, C.-A. (2014). Linguistic Resources for Natural Language Processing. Ph.D. dissertation, A. I. Cuza University, Faculty of Computer Science, Iaşi.

Popa, C. (2010). FDG Parser for Romanian language. Master thesis, A. I. Cuza University, Faculty of Computer Science.

Przepiórkowski, A., Krynicki, Z., Dębowski, L., Woliński, M., Janus, D. and Bański, P. (2004). A search tool for corpora with positional tagsets and ambiguities. In Proceedings of the Fourth International Conference on Language Resources and Evaluation, LREC 2004, p. 1235–1238.

Sproat, R. and Shih, C. (1988). Prenominal Adjectival Ordering in English and Mandarin. In J. Blevins, J. Carter (Eds.), Proceedings of NELS 18, Amherst, MA: GLSA, vol. 2, p. 465–489.

Association for Computational Linguistics
209 N. Eighth Street
Stroudsburg, Pennsylvania 18360

CURRAN ASSOCIATES INC.
proceedings.com

ISBN 978-1-7138-1257-9